Nuggets of Gold

by

Rev. Bud Robinson

First Fruits Press
Wilmore, Kentucky
2015

Nuggets of Gold by Bud Robinson

Published by First Fruits Press, © 2015
Previously Published by Pentecostal Publishing Company, [193-?]

ISBN: 9781621712022 (print), 9781621712015 (digital)

Digital version at
http://place.asburyseminary.edu/firstfruitsheritagematerial/97/

Robinson, Bud 1860-1942
    Nuggets of gold / by Bud Robinson.
    122 pages ; 21 cm.
    Wilmore, Ky. : First Fruits Press, ©2015.
    Reprint. Previously published: Louisville, KY : Pentecostal
    Publishing Company, [193-?].
    ISBN: 9781621712022 (pbk.)
    1. Homiletical illustrations. I. Title.
    BV4225 .R62 2015   248

Cover design by Amelia Hegle

First Fruits Press
The Academic Open Press of Asbury Theological Seminary
204 N. Lexington Ave., Wilmore, KY 40390
859-858-2236
first.fruits@asburyseminary.edu
asbury.to/firstfruits

NUGGETS OF GOLD

BY

REV. BUD ROBINSON

PENTECOSTAL PUBLISHING COMPANY
LOUISVILLE, KENTUCKY.

NUGGETS OF GOLD.

A RESPECTABLE POLE-CAT.

A respectable skunk one day met
A young chap a smokin' a cigarette.
Just one whiff of the odor as he went to flee;
"Gee whiz!" said the skunk, "that beats me."

And with his bristles all up like he was going
    to war,
He met a preacher with a long cigar.
"Great Scott!" said the skunk, "what is this
    I've met?
He smells worse than the chap with the cig-
    arette."

"And now with these 'smellers' a running
    around,
I'll go and bury myself deep in the ground.
I'm ashamed of my name, though a skunk
    I am,
I don't smell as bad as a tobacco-using man."

MY DAILY PRAYER.

"Oh, Lord, give me a back-bone as big as
a saw log, and ribs like the sleepers under
the church floor; put iron shoes on me, and
galvanized breeches. And give me a rhinoc-
erous hide for a skin, and hang a wagon load

5

of determination up in the gable-end of my
soul, and help me to sign the contract to fight
the devil as long as I've got a fist, and bite
him as long as I've got a tooth, and then gum
him till I die. All this I ask for Christ's
sake.   AMEN!"

A salvation from all sin for all men,
Is God's plan for fallen man.

A RESPECTABLE PREACHER.

There's a preacher in the city of considera-
ble note,
Who wears a white tie and a long black
coat.
On Sunday he preaches long and loud,
But on Monday he chews and smokes with
the crowd.

This distinguished Divine is a great Bible
teacher,
But, great Scott! who loves to smell a
preacher?
He feeds his people "skimmed milk and
cider,
But this splendid gentleman is a billy-goat
rider.

He sneers at Holiness and makes it a joke,
But at night he's down town riding the goat.

The goat smells bad—and so does the preacher,
But which smells the worst of these two
creatures?

WHAT IS A NEW TESTAMENT CHRISTIAN?

Why, beloved, a New Testament Christian
is a human being with wisdom enough to be
wise and with humility enough to be humble, and with grace enough to be a saint.

THE JOY WAGON.

Some morning you may get up and feel
like your Heavenly Father was dead and
hadn't left you a nickel, but before you get
through with family prayers, Jesus will
come and whisper in your ear that the "Joy
Wagon" is just around the corner, and may-
be by the time it turns the corner a front
wheel will run off and an axle break, and a
whole wagon load of joy will roll out right
into your front yard.

WHAT CHRISTIAN PERFECTION WILL NOT DO.

Christian perfection will not make an A.
M. graduate out of you, but thank the Lord,
it will enable you to make the best use possible of what sense you have. It will not keep
you from snoring in your sleep, but it will
enable you to wake up in a good humor every
morning.

THE NAZARENE PUBLISHING HOUSE.
I have found by observation
That our House of Publication
Carries out its reputation
As a soul-saving station.
And as a Bureau of Information,
On the line of Full Salvation,
It's' the finest in the Nation,
Or in all of God's creation.

BEFORE I WAS CONVERTED.
Before I was converted I could neither write nor read a word, but I met Jesus and He reached down and pulled me up out of a life of sin, and set me down in the Kingdom of grace, and I could read my title clear to a mansion in the skies.

REPENTANCE.
Repentance is a bitter cup to drink out of. But I have found out that God always gives you the worst He has, first. Thank God it gets better and better every day and every hour. But the devil always gives the best that he has first, and it gets worse and worse every day and every hour. I have seen the young man with a tailored suit this year smoking Havana cigars and drinking the best wine, next year he wore a hand-me-down and smoked the old "Virginia cheroot," three for five cents, and drank bust-

head whiskey. By the next year he was down on his uppers, cleaning out spit-toons for a morning "eye-opener."

BEFORE AND AFTER.

Before the war the preachers preached Socrates, Cicero, and the Queen of England. During the war they cussed the Kaiser. After the war they preached the Peace Treaty and the League of Nations, and after that blowed over then along came the Inter-Church World, and that died and they owed Nine Million Dollars on the funeral expenses, but thank the Lord, we Nazarenes don't owe a nickel on it! Jesus said, "Let the dead bury their dead. . . . but come thou and follow me."

UNBELIEF.

Unbelief is hard on the fellow that has got it, and everybody else that he turns it loose on. In all my travels I have never seen a man that got shouting happy in telling us what he did not believe, but I have seen some precious old country mothers, that never saw their name in a county paper, and never read a book on Astronomy, that years ago discovered the "Morning Star" and it lifted them above the fog and mists of this old world, and I have seen them shout their bonnets off in telling what they believed.

THE STRANGEST DISEASE IN THE WORLD.

Pride is the only disease that is known to the human family that makes everybody sick but the fellow that's got it. When you see a man with a bad case of the swell-head and swaggers, you feel like that you will have to order a bottle of smelling salts.

UNANSWERED PRAYER.

When you hear a fellow pray with that old battle-whang and say, "Oh, Lord, I am just a poor weak worm of the dust," yes, he is, and nine times out of ten, he is a tobacco-worm, and smells like a tobacco factory.

THE THREE MEALS.

The three meals victuals represents the three experiences. Breakfast stands for Justification, Dinner stands for Sanctification and Supper stands for Glorification.

THE THREE NOTHINGS.

The Higher Critics commonly known as the Evolutionists tell us that God didn't create man, that he brought himself into existence by evolution, or he comes from nothing. The Christian Scientists come along and tell us that there is no matter, there is nothing but mind, and therefore we are nothing. And the Annihilationists come along and tell us we are going to die and be blotted out of existence, and are going to nothing. So there it is now in plain words— we come from nothing, and we are nothing, and are going to nothing.

PATRIOTISM.

My mother was a Presbyterian by faith and believed in patriotism. She kept the United States flag in sight about all the time. The one mother used was not made out of cloth, but it was surely the real thing. Mother would get a black jack about three feet long, and while she put the stripes on us we saw the stars, and the red, white and blue immediately would appear on the surface. There is the United States Flag, for it is made up of stars and stripes and red, white and blue, and we sure had the goods.

NO DIFFERENCE.

There is no difference between the Methodists and Presbyterians. The Methodist knows he has got it, but is afraid he will lose it, the Presbyterian knows he can't lose it, but he is afraid he hasn't got it.

There is no difference between the Universalists and the Unitarians. I thought for, years that there was, but I find out that there is not. The Universalists teach that God is too good to damn a sinner, and the Unitar-

ians teach that a sinner is too good to be
damned, so when the doctrine is boiled down
and skimmed and analyzed, there is no difference in their teaching; they both propose
to get a sinner into Heaven without being
regenerated or sanctified.

There is no difference between the North
and South. We used to think that there was
a big difference, but we have found out there
is none. Well, the difference is only this: Up
north they wear suspenders, they eat pea-
nuts, and chew gum. Down south they wear
galluses, and eat gubers, and chaw wax.

There is no difference at all between the
rich and the poor. We thought for years,
that there was, but we found out there is not.
The rich have so much and enjoy it so little;
while the poor have so little and enjoy it so
much. So the reader will see that there is
no difference between the rich and poor.

THE SOLUTION FOR THE H. C. L.

One of the problems of life has been with
the laboring man as to how to make both
ends meet. We have discovered how it can
be done, and we gladly give it to the reader.
The way to make both ends meet, is to have
Ox tail soup for dinner and cold boiled
tongue for supper. The reader will see at a
glance that this makes both ends meet.

READY ANSWERS.

A good woman said to the writer one day, while we were eating dinner. "Why, Brother Robinson, do you drink coffee all the time?" I said, "No, Sister, I don't, I never drink it only at meal time."

Upon another occasion a lady said to me, "Brother Robinson, how in the world can you profess to be sanctified and drink coffee?" I told her kindly that I would show her exactly how it was done. I proceeded to put in a spoonful of sugar and pour in a little cream and stirred it up nicely and turned it up and drank it, then I set the cup down and looked up and smiled and said, "Now Sister, that is the way I do it."

While preaching in the First M. E. Church in Chicago, Ill., one Sunday morning, in my preaching I made the statement that there is not a mystery in the Bible. A gentleman jumped to his feet, and shouted, "hold on there, Bro. Robinson." I said, "Brother I am holding on, what is it?" He said, "What are you going to do with the he-goat that come from the west and never touched the ground?" I said, "Why, Brother, as he comes by I will hang my hat on one of his horns and put my collar and tie on him, and I will have an unregenerated sinner, just like

you are. Will you please sit down?" And
he said, "I will," and caflop, he went. Three
days later he was at the altar and prayed
through to victory. He said he had been a
smart-alec in Chicago for ten years, picking
up preachers, and that if I hadn't knocked
him out, he probably wouldn't have been
saved.

Thank God for a Church home where we
can preach and pray and sing and shout, and
nobody can come around and tell us to "cut
it out."

When you see a fellow riding the goat, you
may put it down, that he is not very busy following the Lamb. When a man gets busy
following the Lamb, he has no time to ride
the goat.

We have seen some amusing sights on the
big camp grounds of this country. Here is
what I mean. Sometimes the big preachers
come out to look on. He wears a long black
coat sweeping his knees, buttoned up in front
straight as a gun-stick, with a silk hat on
the back of his head, and looking over the
rims of his glasses, and stepping as high as
a blind horse in new ground, and finally will
kindly sidle up to us and ask us if we think
that conversion is gradual or instantaneous.
Of course we tell him it must be instanta-

neous, that God could not gradually pardon a sinner. He sometimes will look off into the open space and turn and walk away, and as far as we can see he is as ignorant of the New Birth as Nicodemus of old.

DR. DANIEL STEELE ON SANCTIFICATION.

The late Dr. Daniel Steele, of Boston, Mass., who was one of the ripest scholars of Methodism on either side of the ocean, made this remarkable statement. He said: "The doctrine and experience of entire sanctification is the grand depositum of the skies and is lodged with the people called Methodists. It is a nugget of pure gold, but is blackened by the smoke of prejudice, and in the hands of its custodians, they are in danger of selling it to the junk man for old iron."

The sainted Bishop Joyce said just before he fell dead at the Red Rock Camp, that "Holiness is God's proposition to get the devil out of a man."

OUR TEACHING ON THE SIN QUESTION.

We don't teach that you can get so much grace that you could not sin if you wanted to, but we do teach that you can get so much grace that you don't want to sin, and don't have to. Don't you see the difference now between what we teach and what some folks say we teach? Don't you think it is wonderful to be so fixed that the devil can't make you do the thing if you don't want to do it?

A CHURCH WITHOUT A REVIVAL.

A Church that can't have an old-fashioned Holy Ghost revival of heartfelt religion is an institution without an inspiration, and membership in such an institution means "Oh, thou man of God, there is death in the pot." When you boil that down and skim it and analyze the skimmings, it means "Churchanity without Christianity," and a salvation without regeneration, and Christianity without Christ.

THE DEVIL COMES AROUND.

I was having some pretty hard struggles one morning over some of the hard places of life, and the devil sneaked around and said, "You are having a pretty hard time serving the Lord," and I said, "Well, what about when I served you? Don't you remember that the knees were out of my breeches, the elbows were out of my shirt, and the toes were out of my boots, and I had no socks on, and I had no coat to put on. I had nowhere to go, and nobody loved me. But I met Jesus and He pulled me up out of your kingdom and set me down in His. Just look what I got now. Don't you see I made the greatest exchange in all existence when I traded off you for Jesus?" The devil sneaked around the corner, and I never saw him for a week.

TWO SHORTCOMINGS.

If the reader would turn to Romans 3:23 he would hear the Apostle say, "All have sinned and come short of the glory of God." There is where the sinner comes short, and he is the eternal loser. But if the reader would turn over now and read Hebrews 4:1, he gets another idea of coming short. Paul said, "Let us therefore fear, lest a promise being left us of entering into his rest, any of you should seem to come short of it." Here is the danger of the Church member coming short.

WHAT I GOT FROM ADAM AND ME.

Through Adam's disobedience I got carnality, through my own disobedience I got guilt and condemnation. Paul said in Rom. 6:23, "The wages of sin is death." That is what I got for what I did. But in Rom 8:6, Paul said, "To be carnally minded is death." That is what I got from Adam, so Adam and I hung a double death up over my head, and the only way to get rid of what I did, is to go to Eph. 2:1. Paul said, "You hath he quickened who were dead in trespasses and in sin." There I got rid of what I had done,

and that blotted out Romans 6:23, until the
"wages of sin" is not charged up to me any
longer. But I still had that thing hanging
over my head, that I got from Adam. Now
I go to Romans 6:6 where Paul said, "Knowing this that our old man is crucified with
him that the body of sin might be destroyed." There the reader will see that I got
something that delivered me from Romans
8:6. That brings out two works of grace.
For in Eph. 2:1 I was "Quickened and made
alive," and Romans 6:6, I was "Crucified and
put to death." So Conversion is a making
alive process and sanctification is a killing
process.

THE NUMBER THREE.

Stands first for God the Father, God the
Son and God the Holy Ghost, or the Trinity.

It stands for the world and the flesh and
the devil.

It stands for a trinity of graces—Hope,
Faith and Love.

It stands for a trinity of evils—the lust of
the flesh, the lust of the eye, and the pride of
life.

It stands for the threefold salvation in
Luke 1:77. We have a salvation by the re-
misison of our sins. In 2 Thess. 2:13 we
have a salvation through sanctification of

the Spirit and belief of the truth. In 2 Tim. 2:10 we have a salvation with eternal glory.

It stands for the three *places* of abode. In Gen. 19:17 we have the city of Sodom, or the life of sin. We have the plains, or the life of justification, and we have the mountain top life, or the experience of sanctification.

It stands for the three mountains—Mount Sinai, Mount Calvary and Mount Zion. Mt. Sinai stands for conviction, Mt. Calvary for justification and Mt. Zion for holiness.

We have the three *excepts*. In Luke 13:3, "Except ye repent, ye shall all likewise perish." In Matt. 18:3, "Except ye be converted and become as a little child, ye shall not enter into the kingdom of heaven." In Matt. 5:20, 5 "*Except* your righteousness shall exceed the righteousness of the scribes and Pharisees, ye shall in no case enter into the kingdom of heaven."

We have the three *withouts*. In Heb. 11:6, "But without faith it is impossible to please him." In Heb. 9:22, "Without shedding of blood is no remission of sins." In Heb. 12:14, "Without holiness no man shall see the Lord."

We have the three *resurrections* performed by Jesus. In Luke 8:54, 55, He raised Jairus' daughter. In Luke 7:11 to 15, he raised the widow's son, and in St. John 11:43, he raised Lazarus to life.

In Luke 11:5, we have the man going to his friend to borrow three loaves.

In St. John 10:11, we have Christ the Good Shepherd; and in Heb. 13:20, we have Christ the Great Shepherd. In First Peter 5:4, we we have Christ the Chief Shepherd.

The three great facts in the life of Abraham—God promised and Abraham believed, and then God called and Abraham went, and God asked and Abraham gave.

The three great battles fought by Abraham was, first, to give up his father, second, to give up his son Isaac, the third to give up his nephew Lot.

Everything that the devil can't counteract he seeks to counterfeit; and everything that he can neither counteract nor counterfeit he seeks to destroy, therefore, he sought the young child's life that he might destroy him.

It takes the same divine power to bring a sinner from death to life as it took to bring Jesus Christ from death to life.

The reason that God the Father forsook Jesus Christ while He was dying on the Cross was because Jesus took the place of a sinner, and He died like a sinner dies without God, for Jesus could not take the place of a sinner and then die like a Christian. He must needs die alone with the frowns of a sin-avenging God in his face and a dark sun over his head. Great God, think of the death of a lost soul!

The martyrs said we can burn but we can't turn. They also said we can die but we can't deny. No man is a sinner saved by grace; if he is saved by grace he is not a sinner and if he is a sinner he is not saved by grace.

God's grace is sufficient. God did not keep Daniel out of the lions' den, but thank God he did keep him in the lions' den.

A Christian is on the old Gospel Ship and as she sails over life's rough seas if a storm comes up and the Christian becomes excited and jumps overboard God is under no obligations to keep the whales from swallowing him. But if he stays aboard during the storm God is duty bound to bring that vessel safe to the shores of eternal bliss.

You cannot have sin and holiness at the same time. If you have sin you have not got holiness, and if you have got holiness you have not got sin; for they don't both stay in the same hide at the same time. God's remedy for SIN is not pardon but crucifixion, and if the Old Man has been crucified and the body of sin destroyed you have scriptural holiness.

In John 3:16: "For God so loved the world, that he gave his only begotten Son, that whosoever believeth in him should not perish, but have everlasting life." In Eph. 5:25: "Christ so loved the church, and gave himself for it; that he might sanctify it." The reader will see that God the Father so loved, and God the Son so loved. God so loved that he gave His Son and Christ so loved that he gave himself, God so loved the world that he gave His son that the world might be saved, and Christ so loved the church that he gave himself that the church might be sanctified.

The Holy Ghost witnesses to two works of grace for we read in Rom. 8:16, that, "The Spirit himself beareth witness with our spirit, that we are the children of God." We also read in Heb. 10:14, 15, that the Holy Ghost witnesses to our sanctification which makes it very plain that when we are sanctified that we can know it.

WHAT JESUS SAID.

Jesus said many things that he never stopped to explain, but he called and commissioned the Apostle Paul to explain just what He meant. In Luke 13:3, Christ said "Except ye repent ye shall all likewise perish." In 2 Cor. 7:9, 10, Paul said, "Repentance is a godly sorrow for sin." In John 3:3, Christ said, "Ye must be born again." In Col. 1:13, Paul said, "To be born again is to be delivered from the power of darkness and translated into the Kingdom of his dear Son." In Matt. 10:7, Christ said, "Preach the Kingdom of Heaven." In Rom. 14:17, Paul said, "The Kingdom of Heaven is not meat and drink, but righteousness, peace and joy in the Holy Ghost."

TWO MOUNTAIN HOOSIERS.

Bud Robinson and Alvin C. York were born in the great mountains of Tennessee some thirty-five miles apart. The Lord called Bud Robinson to clean up the devil, and He called Alvin C. York to clean up the Kaiser.

AN UNSANCTIFIED PREACHER.

For ten years as a local preacher in the Southern Methodist Church I had something that I did not need, and during those same ten years, I needed something that I did not have. The thing that I had and didn't need was the carnal mind, and the thing that I needed and didn't have was the Baptism with the Holy Ghost and fire. Thank the

Lord! the day that I got rid of the thing that I did not need, I got the thing that I did need!

The reason why we call money dough, is because we need it so much.

DOUBLE WORKS.

Both conversion and sanctification are double works, for in pardon the sinner must be quickened and made alive and at the same time God must blot out the sins that he has committed. In sanctification the believer must be cleansed from carnality and at the same time he must be filled with the blessed Holy Ghost. This makes both pardon and purity double works of grace.

TWO RESTS.

Again we have the two rests spoken of. In Matt. 11:28, 29, 30, Christ says, "Come unto me, all ye that labor and are heavy laden, and I will give you rest." The reader will see that there is a rest promised to the heavy laden, or if you please, the guilty sinner; but Christ offers to this same person another rest on another condition, that is, if he will take the yoke of Christ and learn of Him, he is to receive the second rest. That is what St. Paul meant in Heb. 4:9, when he said, "There remaineth therefore a rest to the people of God." But in the third verse of the same chapter he said, "We which have believed do enter into rest." He did not say we which have not believed but thank the Lord, we which have believed do enter in.

TWO WAYS.

In the 35th chapter of Isaiah's prophecy we have the two ways—first the highway, and second the way. In the highway. The way in the highway was called the way of holiness. The new birth brings the sinner up out of a horrible pit of sin on to the beautiful highway of righteousness, and then he finds the way that was in the way, for he said, "An highway shall be there, and a way, and it shall be called the way of holiness, and the unclean shall not pass over it."

TWO PRAYERS.

Two prayers offered by Jesus for the two works of grace. In Luke 23:34, Christ said, "Father, forgive them; for they know not what they do." In John 17:17, Christ said to His Father, "Sanctify them through thy truth; thy word is truth." Here are the two prayers offered by our Lord for the two works of grace.

TWO BAPTISMS.

In Matt. 3rd chapter, we have the two baptisms. First, with water, and second,

with the Holy Ghost. We also see the two
baptizers—John and Jesus. Their baptisms
were applied at two different times. We also
see the two different elements used and used
for two different purposes; water baptism
standing for regeneration and the Baptism
with the Holy Ghost standing for scriptural
holiness. There are the two works of grace.

DOUBLE PRAYER.

We next notice that King David offered a
double *prayer*. In the 51st Psalm, and first
and second verses, he first prayed, "Have
mercy upon me O Lord and blot out my
transgressions." He prayed in the second
verse that God would cleanse him from his
sin.

DOUBLE REMEDY.

As sin is a double tragedy God in His goodness provided a double remedy through the
atonement that was made by our blessed
Christ on the Cross. In Rom. 5:8, 9, 10, we
read, "But God commendeth his love toward
us, in that, while we were yet sinners, Christ
died for us. Much more then, being now justified by his blood, we shall be saved from
wrath through him." Here the reader will
see a perfect redemption for a perfect justification. We read in Heb. 13:12 that Jesus
also made a sacrifice of Himself on the Cross

that He might "sanctify the people with his own blood." So the reader will see here a double atonement. Man has a double need because sin is two-fold, inbred and outbroken. Carnality on the *bottom* and *transgression* at the top. One must be pardoned and the other must be cleansed.

TWO TOUCHES.

In Mark 8:23 to 25 we have the two touches for the blind man. The Lord touched his eyes once and he saw men as trees walking; and he touched him the second time and he saw every man clearly.

TWO WILLS.

We also have the two wills of God in regard to the salvation of men. In second Peter 3:9 we read that it is God's will that sinners repent; and we also read in First Thess. 4:3, that it is God's will that believers shall be sanctified.

TWO ESCAPES.

In Gen. 19:17 we have the two escapes; the first one was from the City of Sodom to the plains, and the second one was from the plains to the mountain.

TWO CROSSINGS.

We have the two crossings of the Israelites; first, we have the crossing of the Red

Sea. That crossing brought them from the bondage of Pharaoh to the wilderness; and then after their wanderings for forty years we have them making the second crossing, and at this crossing they crossed the River Jordan and that brought them into the Canaan Land. There are the three countries— Egypt, the wilderness, and the Land of Canaan. One crossing between Egypt and the wilderness, and one crossing between the wilderness and the Land of Canaan.

TWO GATES.

In Isaiah 62:10, we have the two gates. The Old Prophet said "Go through, go through the gates."

I heard a great preacher say standing on a platform of a great camp ground that the Church of which he was a member had taken the fire out of hell, the gold out of heaven, the blood out of the Atonement, the inspiration out of the Bible, and God out of Christ. Fifteen hundred people were there who belonged to his church and not less than 25 preachers of the same denomination and not a one disputed the statement.

No sane man can read very far in the Bible without being perfectly convinced in his mind that the God that is revealed in the Holy Scriptures loves holiness and hates sin.

Again, no man can read very far in the Bible without finding out that the devil that is revealed in the Holy Scriptures loves sin and hates holiness. If we know that God loves holiness and hates sin, and the devil loves sin and hates holiness it will be no trouble for any man that wants to know the truth and do the right to tell who to line up with and where to take his stand.

TWO POWERS.

Again, the two greatest powers that are known to God, men or devils are holiness and worldliness, and these two great powers are knocking at the door of every church on earth and it is owing to who we open the door to as to how the institution is going to go, for if we open to the world then the world will come in and take charge and leaven the whole lump, and finally land the whole cargo in the pit of eternal damnation. But on the other hand, if we open the doors of the Church to scriptural holiness, holiness will come in and leaven the whole lump and finally land the whole cargo on the shores of eternal bliss.

Again, we find that it is God's plan and will and purpose to save the world through the church, and if that be so, then what kind of a church can the Lord use to save the

world through? Can He take a worldly
church and save the world through it? Of
course not; you know God could not save the
world through a church that is full of the
world. That being the case, what kind of a
church can He use? We answer that God
can only save the world through a holy
church.

We find that the hope of the church is in
the amount of holiness that there is in it;
and while that is true, the danger of the
church is in the amount of worldliness that is
in it. Holiness is the hope of the church and
worldliness is the danger of the church.

When you see a preacher getting his
breath through a pipe stem you are not surprised if you see the smoke coming out of
his nose.

There was a time when God's priests
burned sweet incense to create a sweet perfume before the Lord their God, but things
have changed so the preachers tell us and
they say that we are living in a new age and
nowadays they burn Bull Durham tobacco
before the Lord to create a stink in the nos-
trils of their God. Can't you see the change?

The difference between the holiness folks
and the other folks, is clearly seen. The holiness folks are so busy following the Lamb
that they have no time to ride the goat;

while the other folks are so busy riding the goat they have no time to follow the Lamb.

SOME OF THE MARKS OF THE GREATNESS OF ABRAHAM.

Some men were faithful but Abraham was the Father of the Faithful. Some men have founded a nation but Abraham was the Father of one. Some men have been friendly with God, but Abraham was the friend of God. God promised and Abraham staggered not through unbelief but was strong in the faith giving glory to God, and being fully persuaded that what God had promised He was able to perform. God called and Abraham went out, not knowing whither he went. But thank God, Abraham knew with whom he went. God asked and Abraham gave his beautiful Son Isaac. God promised and Abraham believed, God called and Abraham went, God asked, and Abraham gave.

Three ladies were discussing the wonderful traits of character of their pastors, and while two told of the greatness of their pastors, the third listened and when they got through she told them her pastor could dive deeper, and stay down longer, and then come up drier than any man in the nation. She evidently won the case.

It was God's will and plan and purpose to

take the Israelites and make of them a nation of Priests; but they rejected God and made of themselves a nation of peddlers.

It was God's purpose in establishing the United States as a nation to take this nation of people and make them a nation of saints, and let the world behold what God could do, but as a nation we have rejected the blessed Holy Ghost and behold we have become a nation of sinners.

God's dealings with man are not always understood, but they are always right. God did not keep Daniel out of the lions' den but thank God, he did keep him in the lions' den. What he said to Paul he had said to Daniel, "My grace is sufficient for thee." So Daniel went in but Daniel came out and raised a mighty shout and knocked the devil out. Glory to Jesus!

The thing that I need is to learn how to do the right thing in the right way and do it at the right time. That will make me a great success in the vineyard of the Lord; but if I do the right thing at the wrong time I have defeated myself; or if I do the right thing in the wrong way I still have defeated the object that I had in view. Help me Lord, as thy servant, to do the right thing in the right way and do it at the right time. Amen.

St. Peter said, "Beloved, think it not

strange concerning the fiery trial which is
to try you, as though some strange thing
happened unto you. 1 Peter 4:12.

"For it pleased the Father that in him
should all fulness dwell." Col. 1:19.

"For in him dwelleth all the fullness of the
Godhead bodily." That is Jesus. Col. 2:9.

"In whom are hid all the treasures of wisdom and knowledge." That is Jesus. Col. 2:3.

Beloved, if you have prayed through that
makes you a P. T., and that will give you a
level head, a big soul, a good heart and a loving disposition. Don't you think that is
worth striving after?

"Put on the whole armour of God, that ye
may be able to stand against the wiles of the
devil." Eph. 6:11.

Beloved, if you have obeyed the above
Scriptures you have the face of a saint and
the heart of a martyr, and that will give you
the courage of a hero and the endurance of
a soldier.

"Wherefore take unto you the whole armour of God, that ye may be able to with-
stand in the evil day, and having done all, to
stand." Eph. 6:13. Beloved, if you have
obeyed the above Scripture that will give you
the tears of a Jeremiah, the fire of an Isaiah,
the vision of an Ezekiel, the music of a David and the wisdom of a Solomon.

"Stand therefore, having your loins girt
about with truth, and having on the breast-
plate of righteousness; and your feet shod
with the preparation of the gospel of peace."
Eph. 6:14, 15.

Oh, beloved, if you can say amen to the
above scripture you will have the purity of
the white dove and your life will be the very
unselfishness of sunshine. You will meet the
obstacles of life with the patience of a Job
and come out more than conqueror in all the
battles of life. Your presence in the community will be like the perfume of the flowers.

"Above all, taking the shield of faith,
wherewith ye shall be able to quench all the
fiery darts of the wicked." Eph. 6:16. The
shield of faith is that mysterious, inexplain-
able something that protects the child of God
from the fiery darts of the devil. Faith is
the unseen hand that reaches God and is
guided by that peculiar something that we
call prayer. So we see that prayer and faith
are inseparable; they are united in holy wed-
lock and what God has joined together let
not man put asunder.

"And take the helmet of salvation, and the
sword of the Spirit, which is the word of
God; praying always with all prayer and
supplication in the Spirit, and watching

thereunto with all perseverance and supplication for all saints." Eph. 6:17, 18.

There is enough Gospel in these two verses to save a nation, and power enough to save the lowest sinner on the face of the earth, and glory enough to fill the heart of every child of God. The helmet of salvation is that something that covers the saint as a garment. It is eternal life; it is the robe of righteousness; it is the garments of salvation. The sword of the Spirit, Paul says, is the word of God. In Heb. 4:12, Paul says, "For the word of God is quick and powerful, and sharper than any two-edged sword, piercing even to the dividing asunder of soul and spirit, and of the joint and marrow, and is a discerner of the thoughts and intents of the heart." There is power enough to make the sinner as white as snow, the believer as red as blood and give him a vision as clear as the blue sky, and make his life as straight as a gun stick, and make him so hot if the devil or any of his crowd sits down on him he will burn a blister on him.

It is a thousand times better to know the Rock of Ages than it is to know the ages of the rocks.

I have seen many big preachers with lots of titles to their names and not a fish on their strings.

Every theory of the doctrine and experience of entire sanctification that denies the second work of grace makes provision to keep the Old Man in the heart and life.

The theory of conversion and entire sanctification taking place at the same time is unscriptural and unreasonable, for God cannot sanctify a guilty sinner, but must pardon him. The American Church doesn't teach or preach or practice or live or profess the experience of entire sanctification. "Nuff said," as C. W. Ruth says.

GROWTH THEORY.

The growth theory of the doctrine and experience of entire sanctification is unscriptural, unreasonable, unbelievable and unthinkable; for good common sense teaches us that growth does not change the moral condition of anything. The justified believer can no more grow the inbred sin out of his heart than the guilty sinner can grow the outbroken sin out of his heart. The first must be pardoned and the second must be cleansed.

SUPPRESSION THEORY.

The theory of suppression is misleading and is a deception of the devil. The devil is the daddy of such teaching, for the Old Man in the heart held down is as distasteful to

the Lord as when he is sitting up, or even
standing up. What is the difference? Nothing could be more displeasing to the Lord
than to see one of His children spending his
days in trying to hold the Old Man down.
God said, "Put off the old man with his
deeds," and not hold him down with his
deeds. The Lord said, "Put off therefore,
the old leaven." He said, "Put off the Old
Man." He said, "Crucify the Old Man," and
He also said, "Destroy the body of sin."

DEATH THEORY.

Again, the death theory of entire sanctification is unscriptural and misleading; it is
not possible that death could have anything
to do with the sanctification of a man's soul.
The old Book says that death is the last ene-
my that we are to overcome, and who on
earth but a false teacher could have the
cheek to stand up in a church and point the
people to that grim monster death, for the
beautiful experience of entire sanctification,
that the Bible says we are to have in this
life.

SECOND BLESSING THEORY.

There is just one theory of sanctification
that is scriptural and reasonable, and that is
the second-blessing theory. We don't get it
at the new birth, and we must have it to get

into heaven; so anywhere we get it between
conversion and heaven makes it a second
work of grace. Well, amen. Every person
that I have ever heard say that holiness
would split the church was the crowd that
did not have it.

The Nazarenes are a very sensible people;
they have entirely too much sense to chew
anything that they are afraid to swallow,
therefore they only chew at meal time and
swallow everything that they chew. Good
for us.

There was a day that I remember well
when the American Church demanded of
their members a new heart, but behold, the
day has come when they only demand a few
new habits, and they are very tame on that
line. If Jesus tarries for another generation what will they demand!

I never saw a Church program that had a
place on it for an altar service or for an altar
call, or a committee of workers to pray them
through at the altar, and I have wondered
why.

There was a day in the American Church
when the woman that was the ablest in prayer and lived the most godly life was the lead-
er in the Church of which she was a member,
but that day has passed; and today the most
popular woman in the Church is the one with

the largest bulldog with the crookedest legs, the crookedest pug nose, and with a bobtail and a brass collar on his neck. Gentlemen, she is at the head of the institution and no make believe.

The preachers tell us that we live in a new age and I believe it, for when I was a sinner if a fellow stole anything they called him a rascal or a thief, but behold, nowadays when a man steals anything they tell us that he has kleptomania, and when a woman takes what does not belong to her that she is only a shoplifter. Don't you see the difference?

Here is another difference that proves that we are living in a new age. When Adam got his first suit of clothes the Lord had to skin a four-legged animal to get his suit, but when I got my last suit a two-legged animal skinned me. Don't you see the great change, and don't you think the change is simply wonderful?

Some thirty years ago General William Booth, the founder of the Salvation Army, said that the day will come both in Europe and America, when the churches will substitute church membership for the new birth, and the activities of the Church for the gifts of the Holy Ghost. "Then," said he, "we will have a salvation without regeneration and a Christianity without Christ. The dear old

General lived to see his own prophecies fulfilled.

Lorenzo Dow said in the days in which he lived that there was a people in his country that had the strangest doctrine in the world; they were called the "Hard-shell Baptists." He said their doctrine was this: "You can and you can't, you will and you won't, and you will be damned if you do, and you will be damned if you don't." This is their teaching according to Mr. Dow.

Some wonderful things that God used St. Peter to do on the day of Pentecost. He used him to open the Kingdom to the Jews. Sorry so many rejected it, but thank God for the few that accepted it. Several years later God used him to open the kingdom to the Gentiles at the home of Cornelius. These are the two great things in the life and labours of the beloved St. Peter.

Some beautiful things that some great men have said about the life of the great Apostle St. Paul. General William Booth, the great warrior and founder of the Salvation Army, said of him that from the day that he met Christ on the Damascus road that he never wobbled. Dr. Daniel Steele, of Boston, who was one of the ripest scholars of Methodism on earth's side of the great old blue, said of St. Paul, that from the day that he met Christ and came forward for prayers in the middle of the big road that he never wavered. The late Dr. W. B. Godbey, of world-wide fame, said of St. Paul, from the day that St. Paul met Christ on the Damascus road and Christ pulled him off of his horse and brought him forward for prayers that he never flickered. Dr. Henry Morrison, who is the Editor of The Pentecostal Herald and also the President of Asbury College, Wilmore, Ky., who is of world-wide fame, and of his preaching ability has no equals on the face of the earth, said of St. Paul, that from the day that St. Paul met the Son of God on the Damascus road and shouted, "Who art thou, Lord?" Christ answered back to him, "I am Jesus whom thou persecuteth," that from that hour till the day of his death he stood like Gibraltar.

The Reverend William H. Huff, who is of national reputation as an evangelist and preacher, who is also a great reader, traveler and thinker, said of St. Paul that from the day that the shaft of light from heaven unhorsed him and brought him to the altar of prayer, until the day when Nero's sword flashed in the air and St. Paul's head dropped into the sand, that he stood like he had rock-ribs under his feet. Thank the Lord, for these tributes from such godly and great

men concerning the greatest holiness warrior that ever trod this earth.

When the sinner takes the first step from
a life of sin to the life that is eternal and
meets God at the place of prayer and his
guilt is rolled away, his next step is toward
the altar of consecration. If there he meets
God's condition and he is sanctified, his next
step is toward the marriage Supper of the
Lamb. Here we see justification, sanctification and glorification. The two first installments are received in this country, and
the third one in the land where there are no
shadows. Glory to God in the highest! I
have received the two first installments and
thank God, I am a candidate for the third.

My soul is on the stretch for the glory
land. I am sick of sin and drifting sand and
on the Rock of Ages I mean to stand.

The inheritance of the child of God here is
what he has as his possessions on this earth,
beside what is coming to him in heaven. He
has God for his Father, Christ for his Savior, the Holy Ghost for his abiding Com-
forter, the redeemed saints of all the ages for
his brothers and sisters, the angels for his
companions in life, the Bible for his waybill
from earth to heaven, and then he has heav-
en for his eternal home. I say that we are
well off. What say you?

"It is impossible to rightly govern the world without God and the Bible."—*George Washington.*

God's angels open locks as easily as his sunbeams open rosebuds."—*H. W. Warner.*

"What makes men good Christians makes them good citizens."—*Daniel Webster.*

"There is no perfect Christian who is not also a perfect patriot:"—*Cardinal Mercier.*

"When the devil comes up and lays down before you a temptation Jesus Christ walks up and lays down the way of an escape by the side of it."—*J. B. McBride.*

The late Dr. P. F. Breese used to say in his preaching: "Get the glory down."

The sainted Dr. C. J. Fowler used to say when we were in an altar service, "Hold steady."

The Rev. C. E. Cornell used to say when we were praying the seekers through at the altar, "All hands lift."

Dr. H. C. Morrison closes his great editorials with these words, "On with the revival."

Rev. John Norberry says, "Keep on believing."

In Gen. 7:1, Noah brought his house into the ark, and in 2 Samuel 6:10, Obededom brought the Ark into his house.

While walking slowly down the street,
A pale-faced lad I chanced to meet;
He passed me by and never spoke,
But blew my face full of tobacco smoke.

Jonah was the first man that ever made a trip in a submarine that we have any account of. He surely was ahead of the Huns.

The night that Daniel stayed in the lions' den is the first real case of lock-jaw that we have on record, and the angel of the Lord went down and shut the lions' mouths and thank God, they could not open them.

In St. John 14:30, Christ said that "The prince of this world cometh and hath nothing in me." We also read in 1st John 4:17, "Because as he is, so are we in this world." The above Scriptures teach us that the devil has no part or lot in Christ or a sanctified soul.

"For many deceivers are entered into the world who confess not that Jesus Christ is come in the flesh." This is a deceiver and an anti-christ. 2 John 1:7. Here is Eddyism, pure and simple, and no make believe about it. Here are the old lady's tracks.

"The difference between the temptation of Jesus and a sinner is seen in this fact: whatever part the carnal mind plays in temptation Jesus never had."—*C. W. Ruth.*

The importance of entire sanctification is seen when we see that the triune God is interested in our sanctification. For God the Father willed it to us. Jesus died that we might have it, and the Holy Ghost witnesses to it.

The doctrine and experience of entire sanctification has the largest place in the Holy Scriptures of any other one subject that is discussed between Genesis and Revelation. Why is this? Because this is the one thing that is essential to get you into Heaven. What is the one thing that you must have to get into Heaven? *Holiness.* Then, let no man or woman try to pass the pearly portals without a holy heart.

THREE GREAT FACTS IN PAUL'S LIFE.

There are three chapters in the New Testament that bring out three great facts. The third chapter of Paul's letter to the Romans is a life-sized photo of the unregenerated world about us. The condition could not be worse than we have here pictured by the inspired Apostle. From the 10th to the 20th verse is the darkest picture in the New Testament.

But if the reader will turn to the third chapter of 1st Corinthians he will find another photo; this time it is of the regenerated believer. The Apostle said that these Corinthian Christians were babes in Christ; but he also said that they were yet carnal; that they were taking the milk of the word but could not take the meat; and that the reason was that they were yet carnal. Babes in Christ and yet carnal, taking the milk and could not take the meat.

Now if the reader will turn to the third chapter of Paul's letter to the Ephesians he will find a life-sized photo of the sanctified saint. From the 14th to the 21st verse we have the most beautiful experience that is described between the lids of the Holy Bible. We have a class of people that understood the length and breadth and depth and heights of the love of God and were filled with all the fulness of God. Here is the high water mark of Christian experience.

Some beautiful clippings from the *Purity Crusader*, written by our beloved Brother J. T. Upchurch, in the October number of 1921:

Oh, the endless endlessness of endless eternity! Can you grasp it?

Have faith in God as you move on through space out into eternity.

There are four subjects that stagger the finite mind—space, eternity, faith, God.

Faith is all but omnipotent, for Jesus said,

"All things are possible to him that believeth." The boundless boundlessness of a boundless faith! Can you grasp it?

If we are to be happy we must both trust God and place confidence in man. To do this, we must have some knowledge of both God and man. Our subject deals alone in having faith in God.

While some people are devoting their time to studying the ages of the rocks, I am busying myself learning about the Rock of Ages, He who holdeth the spiritual and temporal wealth of the world in His hand.

God, the ruler of the Universe, infinite in love, wisdom, knowledge, power, mercy and justice. An absolute monarch, a tender, loving Father. Oh the majesty, grandeur and compassion of God! Whose circumference is nowhere, whose center is everywhere. Can you grasp it?

Faith, that indefinable mysterious something that holds the Universe together. We understand that through faith the worlds were formed by the word of God. Faith, the substance of things hoped for, is possible to every human being, but all may not be capacitated to receive it in the same measure; however, each individual may increase his capacity.

We are told that if we start a train from

the earth running a mile a minute and run it day and night, it would require forty million years to reach the nearest star. The nearest star is in space and there is space beyond that occupied by other stars. God fills all space. Can you grasp it!

As has been previously stated in these columns, faith is an act of the creature as well as the gift of God. It is a grace of the Spirit as well as the gift of the Spirit and we are exhorted to earnestly covet the best gifts.

John Wesley said to a person that had just received the experience of perfect love, God did give you the "second blessing properly so called." He also said, "If there be no such a thing as the second work of grace then we must be content to let sin remain in us till we die.

TOBACCO FACTORIES.

If our nation doesn't rise up in its God-given power and destroy the tobacco factories the tobacco factories will rise up in the power of the devil and destroy this nation.

There is not a preacher in the world of any denomination with brains enough, social standing enough, and spiritual power enough to harmonize and bring together the Church of Jesus Christ and the Bull Durham Tobacco Company. It can't be done. If the

Church will clean up, the tobacco factory will die, but if the Church stays dirty then she will die and the tobacco factory will live.

There has never been a preacher on the face of the earth of any faith that can harmonize the working of a Secret Lodge in their midnight proceeding with his pulpit and the altar of prayer. St. Paul is good authority and he said that it is a "Shame to speak of those things that are done of them in secret."

On Sunday morning of September 11th, Dr. Herbert Rhodes, pastor of the Grace Methodist Episcopal Church in St. Louis, Mo., gave out these startling facts: "We have 32,000 Protestant pulpits vacant in America." He said it was partly because the pews are empty, but it is because the pulpits are empty. You take any one of those 32,000 churches and put a man in it full of faith and the Holy Ghost and he will soon have a house full of men and women to preach to. But why are the pulpits empty? Here are the real facts. The schools are full of German dope and the tobacco factories are running day and night; the land is flooded with secret lodges, and neither German dope, a tobacco factory or a secret lodge can make a preacher of the Gospel of Jesus Christ. There is but one power that is known to man that can make a preacher of the gospel of Jesus Christ and that is the blessed Holy Ghost, and He has well nigh been rejected by the great American Church.

Thus speaketh our Lord to us:
Ye call me master and obey me not,
Ye call me light and see me not,
Ye call me way and walk me not,
Ye call me life and desire me not,
Ye call me wise and follow me not,
Ye call me fair and love me not,
Ye call me rich and ask me not,
Ye call me eternal and seek me not,
Ye call me gracious and trust me not,
Ye call me noble and serve me not,
Ye call me mighty and honor me not,
Ye call me just and fear me not,
If I condemn you blame me not.

—Selected.

In flower gardens we sometimes see flowers of many different shades and colors, but yet they all belong to the same species of flowers. So it is in the Christian life; we see many different graces but they all spring from the one heavenly plant of love. The different graces are only the different manifestations of the one thing. As some one has said, "Joy is love victorious; peace is love at rest; longsuffering is love suffering; patience is love under trial; goodness is love at home; kindness is love at service, faith is love in the conflict; temperance is love on the battle field; endurance is love under marching orders; perseverance is love holding out; justification is love on the witness stand, while sanctification is love with its working clothes on.

When the Lord saves and sanctifies He puts the glory in the soul, the shine on the face and the devil can't rub it off. Glory to Jesus, Brother Will H. Huff says that it looks like a "hardwood finish or a patent leather shine." I say Amen! What do you say about it? Well, that just suits me, I am most tickled to death over what I have got.

The most beautiful thing in all the world is Christian Perfection. It is of such importance that God had Moses to write it in the Law, the Prophet Isaiah wrote it in fire, Jeremiah wrote it in tears, Ezekiel saw it in his wonderful vision, Solomon wrote it in Songs, and King David wrote it in his music. Oh beloved, two works of grace will put the glory in your soul and a shine on your face.

In St. John, the 14th chapter and the 30th verse, our blessed Savior said that, "the prince of this world cometh and hath nothing in me." We also read in first John the

4th chapter and the 17th verse: "And as he is, so are we in this world." Beloved reader, you may rest assured that if there is anything in you that belongs to the devil that he will be around after it. The devil had nothing in Christ and you may be so saved by Christ that there is nothing left in you that the devil can lay claim to.

THE SAINTS' DAILY PRAYER.

Oh Lord, touch my brains that I may think in perfect harmony with thy will, and plan and purpose concerning me. Touch my heart that I may love as my Savior loved lost men. Touch my eyes that I may see the beauty in a life hid with Christ in God. Touch my ears that I may hear thy voice. Touch my very bones and blood and muscles till my whole life will be brought under the power and dominion of the blessed Holy Ghost, and so energize my faith that I can grasp thy hand and walk with thee through a world of sin and finally make the landing on the shores of eternal bliss, and abide with thee and the redeemed forever and ever Amen.

THE FIRST WORK OF THE CHURCH.

The first work of the Church is to give the Gospel to the whole world. If our forty-one million church members were filled with the

Holy Ghost we could evangelize the whole world in this generation.

Divine love gave all and Divine love requires all; therefore, a Bible saint never asks how little can I give and still get to heaven, but how much can I give of what God has given to me? Such a saint never asks how much of my money shall I give to the Lord, but the thing he really asks is, How much of God's money shall I keep for myself? The Bible saint always feels that he is only God's steward.

The Rev. U. E. Harding says, "We have had a world-wide war; why not now have a world-wide revival? and how could we begin it better than with a world-wide love-feast?

Dr. James B. Chapman says, "Education without Christianity is like putting a razor in the hand of a child; the razor is all right but the child does not know how to use it in safety." Christianity corrects the heart and this makes it easier to train and correct the intellect.

If the Peace Council held in Washington, D. C., could have succeeded in extracting the teeth of the dogs of war and making peaceful watch dogs out of them, this would have been the greatest council that has met in a business session in the past thousand years.

We know by experience that a man's religion doesn't save him from paying tax, and
his grocery bill, and the interest on what he
owes. Then, if it doesn't save him from sin,
what is it good for? Wouldn't he be just as
well off without it? And yet thousands of
church members tell us that they sin every
day in word, thought, and deed, and that
they are on the road to heaven. Well now,
hear me just a minute. If a fellow can sin
every day in word, thought and deed, and
still be on the road to heaven, pray tell me
what a fellow would have to do to be on the
road to the other place? Why man, I could
sin every day in word and thought and deed
without any religion at all. My judgment is,
that it does not require any religion at all, to
sin every day. What do you think about it?

When Rev. C. B. Jernigan was district superintendent on the Oklahoma and Kansas
districts of the Church of the Nazarene, he
was one of the apostles of the great Holiness Move; he had two whole states in his
territory, and while working that district he
had the grit, grace and wisdom to put this
kind of an ad in one of the holiness papers:
"A Man Wanted—that can take the bull by
the horns and break his neck, take off his
hide and stretch it for a gospel tent, knock
off his horns and blow them for trumpets,

call the multitudes together and preach full
salvation to them, take the bull's meat and
peddle it out to get money to pay the expenses of the meeting." Hurrah for little
Charlie! He found the man and they got
the goods. Well, Amen.

The Rev. N. B. Herreld, Secretary and
Treasurer of Home Mission and Evangelism,
gave out the plan by which they are to reach
the masses in the United States and interest
them in this great work. He says it can be
done by "Education, agitation, illumination,
organization and realization." I say Amen
to what Bro. Herreld says. As Dr. Morrison
says, "On with the revival!"

Another nugget from the pen of Dr.
J. B. Chapman: "Behold Christ stands at
the door of the Church of the Nazarene ask-
ing to be permitted to come in and use our
forces as His own in the manifestation of
His saving and transforming glory in the
lives of men."

Our moral condition determines our spiritual vision. See Titus 1:15. The man that
is so highly educated that he hasn't got business sense enough to attend to his eternal
destiny before it is too late, was evidently
educated in one of the devil's universities,
and the devil was the acting president.

When I was a boy preacher I used to tell

my congregation that I was going to preach
to their hearts, for I thought in those days
that men's hearts were very soft; but in my
later years I have changed my tactics and
nowadays I tell them that I am going to
preach to their heads, for I have found out
that men's heads are softer than their hearts.

On a large camp ground one morning
while a beautiful testimony meeting was
running and the saints were full of praises
and the glory of God was on the multitude, a
young man arose and began to testify, and
he at once began to leap in the air. He
thanked God that he had no education and
that he was ignorant, and was glad of that.
An old white-haired saint with a beautiful
smile on his face said, "Young man, you
have lots to be thankful for."

Dr. James B. Chapman says, "Oh Christ,
since thou hast stooped to call at the en-
trance of my lonely cot, though embarrassed
for lack of fitness, I shall not bear the
charge of inhospitality, I swing the door
wide, and not content to merely let thee in,
I implore thee, oh come and dwell with me."

THE DIFFERENCE.

The difference between God's people and
the devil's people is just this one little difference and it is so small that many people

say that they can see no difference at all. Well, here is the only difference; God's people are saints and the devil's people are sinners. You see that both words start with the letter s, and both words close with the letter s, but the difference is in the middle of these two most remarkable words.

Every sinner on earth belongs to the devil's hook and ladder brigade, and every round in the devil's ladder begins with the letter d. See how the ladder is made, and that every step leads downward—disobedience, dishonesty, disheartened, drunkenness, disgrace, discouraged, deceptions, despair, despondence, death, damnation. You may read the devil's ladder either up or down and it leads the young man or woman to their eternal ruin.

The difference between the American Church today and what it was when we first knew it, is simply this: forty-two years ago it was a cyclone of fire and glory, and today it is well-nigh a pool of stagnation. The Church has been laid on the table of carnality and sold out to intellectuality and paid for in dead spirituality. The biggest trouble is simply this; the average American preacher is so busy riding the goat that he has no time to follow the Lamb. The Church is lodged and clubbed to death.

REMARKABLE CHAPTER.

The second chapter of Paul's letter to
Titus is one of the most remarkable chapters
in the New Testament for advice to all classes of people of every age. In the first verse
is God's general command; in the second
verse we have his advice to the old men,
which is beautiful; in the third is his instructions to the old ladies; in the fourth and
fifth we find the most remarkable advice and
instructions to the young women that we
find in the New Testament; in the sixth and
seventh and eighth we have his instructions
to the young men; in the ninth and tenth
verses we have his instructions to the servants, and from the eleventh to the fifteenth
we have him giving us a general command
that reaches the old man, the old lady, and
the younger women, and the young men and
the servants. They are all brought into this
one class. This is the only chapter that
takes up each class.

THE SAINTS' FLEET.

The Saints' fleet is one of the strongest
and most beautiful that was ever built; in
fact, this is the only fleet that man knows
anything about that cannot be torpedoed and
sunk. No storm has ever been able to drive
her to the shores, and thank God, she has

never gone on the breakers: she never has to be run into a dry dock, and has never been logged up. No man has ever had to scrape the barnacles off of the bottom of this wonderful fleet. She has plowed the stormy seas for the past ages and is stronger today than ever before; she has landed every passenger that has ever taken passage and stayed aboard, on the shores of eternal deliverance. Of course, when a storm comes up if a passenger jumps overboard this is not the fault of the vessel, and she has no time to stop and haul out the weak-kneed passengers, that would rather take to an open sea than to stay aboard. This fleet is composed of four of the most beautiful vessels that man has ever put his eyes on, and their names tell us of their grandeur, beauty and glory. Here are the names in their regular order: *Friendship, Companionship, Fellowship, Heirship.*

Dr. Edward F. Walker's definition of sanctification as a second work of grace: "Sanctification in the proper sense is a work of grace instantaneously wrought in the person of a believer by the baptism with the Holy Ghost, administered by Jesus Christ, purifying him from all sin and perfecting him in divine love."

Dr. P. F. Breese, the founder of the
Church of the Nazarene, and its first General
Superintendent, said that, "We are debtors
to every man to give him the gospel in the
same measure as we have received it."
Amen. Lord, help us to do it and not disap-
point our founder and our Lord and Savior
Jesus Christ, for God will bless any church
that will try to save the lost of the earth.

STEWARDSHIP.

David Livingston, the great African ex-
plorer, and the man who is looked on as the
greatest missionary that our world has produced in the last thousand years, has said,
"I will place no value on anything I have or
may possess except in relation to the kingdom of God."

The first work of the whole Church is to
give the gospel to the whole world. If that
statement be true, and it is, what kind of a
Church can God use in evangelizing the
world? We only have two kinds of churches
on the face of the whole earth—a holy
church and a worldly church. No sane man
could believe that God could take a worldly
church and use it to save the world. If that
be the case, and it is, then if God saves the
world through the church He must have a
holy church to work through.

Mr. Moody has said, "If you take God into partnership with you, you must make your plans much larger."

It was John Wesley, the founder of Methodism who said, "Make all you can, save all you can, and give all you can."

It was Mr. John Wanamaker that said, "The difference between the clerk who spends all of his salary and the one that saves a part of it is the difference in ten years between the owner of a business and a man out of a job."

Mr. D. L. Moody said, "Some day you will read in the papers that D. L. Moody, of Northfield, is dead. Don't you believe a word of it. At that moment I shall be more alive than I am now. I shall have gone up higher, that is all, out of this old clay tenement into a house that is immortal, a body that death cannot touch, that sin cannot taint; a body fashioned like unto His glorious body. I was born of the flesh in 1837. I was born of the Spirit in 1856. That which is born of the flesh will die, that which is born of the Spirit will live for ever."

God seems to have established His kingdom on earth under the Old Dispensation with three leading characters. We might call them a kind of human trinity; it was

Abraham, Isaac and Jacob. How wonderful God has used those three men in bringing blessings to the human family.

We also find that God has taken three men under the New Dispensation as the three standard bearers in the persons of Peter, James and John. We turn to the Old Testament and it is Abraham, Isaac, and Jacob; and we come to the New and it is always Peter, James and John. I suppose that the two greatest religious teachers that our world has ever produced were Moses and St. Paul; one in the Old Testament and one in the New.

GOLD NUGGETS FROM DR. B. F. HAYNES.

Love, Joy, Peace—these present the work of the Holy Ghost in His sanctifying operation wherein He constitutes character as an inward state. This is a divine adjustment of man with relation to himself.

Longsuffering, Gentleness, Goodness—this is the Spirit's adjustment of man's character toward his fellowman. It is character in its expression toward man.

Faithfulness, Meekness, Temperance—this is the adjustment or regulation of character toward God. Thus is compassed in the glorious fruits of the Spirit, the adjustment of the sanctified toward every possible relation in life; those toward himself, those toward his fellowman, and those toward God.

God's plan of work has always been three-fold. He has always done all that a loving heavenly Father could do by His grace and when grace failed, He did all that could be done by Law, and when Law failed He always brought the sword on the land and accomplished His purpose.

MARKS OF THE GREATNESS OF MAN'S SOUL.

First, it was made by God Himself and that within itself is proof of its greatness.

Second, it was made in the image of God. The soul of man is the only thing in existence that was ever made in God's image.

Third, it was made like God in that it is immortal and will exist forever. You have never seen the grave of man's soul and never will. You could no more find the grave of man's soul than you could find the grave of God Himself.

Fourth, it was made with a capacity to acquire knowledge. The soul of man can know God personally and even know Him better than we know a friend.

Fifth, it was made with a capacity to enjoy companionship and friendship and fellowship. The soul of man is the only part of man that can really love and enjoy the beau-

tiful things that God has created. The soul
fairly revels in oceans and mountains and
hills and rivers. The plains and valleys
from the spring violet to the climbing rose,
and from the carnation to the honeysuckle
vine; from the tiny sprig of grass to the tall-
est oak; from the crickets in the jamb to
the bob-white on the fencing post.

The saint can see God's footprints in the
valleys and his handiwork on the mountain
side. To the real saint there is shouting
ground all the way down the valley and up
the mountain side. None but the fool has
said in his heart "there is no God." The
Psalmist has said, "Day unto day uttereth
speech and night unto night showeth knowledge." How wonderful are thy works, oh,
God, and that my soul knoweth right well.
But O the blindness and stupidity of the sinner. The old Book said that the Devil has
blinded their eyes; like Esau of old they
have sold their birthright. The sinner says
that my soul is not worth saving, I will revel
for a few days in sin and then be blotted
from God's calendar and spend eternity
away from God.

THE SINNER'S OUTLOOK IN LIFE.

A crooked life, a guilty conscience, a dead
soul, a stupefied brain, a life dominated by

lust and the love of money and its evils. A sinner's outlook is no brighter than the black smoke as it curls from the smokestack of the tobacco factory. The Devil has robbed him of his reason, spoiled his manhood, mildewed his hopes, blasted his possibilities, degraded his best intentions, robbed him of his soul and will keep him out of heaven, and finally populate hell with his precious immortal soul that was made in the image of God and fashioned after God Himself. Strange, you say? Yes, so say I, but beloved, there is in this beautiful little country of ours that we call the United States, just sixty-four millions of such creatures today. Strange, you say? Yes, indeed, but the strangest thing about this strange condition is that it is true.

THE OUTLOOK OF THE SAINT.

The saint's outlook is as bright as the face of the God of the universe. He has been born again, then cleansed from all unrighteousness, filled with all the fullness of God, kept by His power, guided with His eye, and upheld by the right hand of His righteousness. His face is toward God and his back to the Devil. He has been taken out of the world and the world has been taken out of him, thank God. When St. Paul said, "I am

crucified to the world and the world unto
me," the saint says, Amen, that is my condition. The devil has never been able to get
up anything down town that is big enough
to get the attention of a New Testament
saint. Of course, when we say New Testament saints we don't mean the common
church member, for they have neither been
taken out of the world or have had the world
taken out of them. They never made a real
Bible profession; they only "hit the trail"
and joined because the multitude was going
in that way.

NUGGETS OF GOLD FROM C. A. McCONNELL.

Heaven and hell wage warfare for the
possession of Man-Soul when He, the Holy
Ghost, comes in, your will has decided for
His occupancy, and His will decides your
life.

When He comes in, He leads gently, yet
persistently, my meditations from things
carnal to things spiritual.

When He comes in I look out upon a world
with the view of Jesus Christ.

As surely as the old man of sin may be
crucified, killed, eradicated, cast out from
the heart of man, so surely does then come
One into that heart to abide. What the Old
Man was not, He is; what the Old Man was,

bears no likeness to what He is. As the old showed himself through your personality, so will He be seen, even using that which the world calls you.

When He comes in free from the bondage of sin and death, and the things I would do, I can do, through Christ who strengtheneth me.

When He comes in there is not only constant growth, but a mellowing and sweetening in ripenesss.

When He comes in, I am no longer my own; I am in bondage unto my brethren. More, I am fettered with every prisoner, and a sufferer with all the afflicted.

When He comes in, trembling before the face of men is replaced with the calm fearlessness of one who stands in the presence and acts upon the command of All Power.

When He comes in, He transfers to the name of Jesus the title of all my possessions, and then passes the eternal possessions of the Son of God over to my name, as the co-inheritor.

When He comes in, He puts "How" 'at the list of questions I had labeled "Why."

When He comes in, I see God's little friends in all living creatures, and pity and gentleness stay my hand from harshness, cruelty or wanton slaying.

When He comes in, I find delight in the presence of children; their harmless frolic, their simple faith, their courage toward life and their quick sympathy, remind me that of such is the kingdom of heaven.

When He comes in, I am glad as it is proven that my brothers misunderstood action was without sin, for He teaches me daily to think no evil.

When He comes in, it is with a marvel of plainness of speech. Not with enticing words of man's wisdom, high-sounding phrases, and words in other tongues to overawe the unlearned, but in the pure gold of simple speech does He bring the heavenly message.

When He comes in, I do not "strike a pose." The Greek expression for that is hypocrite, and He classes hypocrites with liars.

When He comes in, He makes proof of His divine presence in long-suffering—neither strikes back nor runs away. He points me to the thorn marks and the spittle upon the face of Jesus, and I am ashamed that my hands and feet are not also pierced.

When He comes in, that dark future, filled with forebodings and terrors, burst in the bright certainties of eternal blessedness and that unseparated from this present life.

When He comes in, He teaches me the language of heaven, which is, "Let me do this for you;" not the earth language of, "Do this for me."

When He comes in, temptation, however quick her approach, does not sit down upon the throne with desire, for he has taken desire for His own, and He holds her by the hand.

When He comes in, He leads mistake to the altar of forgiveness, and warns her lest she, coming again, bear the face of sin.

When He comes in, He has His way with me as He stays, and His way is the way of purity, peace and power.

When He comes in there may be a call to leadership, but I will understand that the greatest procession three worlds ever knew, was led by a Man bearing a cross.

"Be a failure for God?" No! If you are a failure you will be damned. God's plan contains no provision for failures. After His resurrection Jesus proclaimed: "All power is given unto me," and "Go ye," and "Lo! I am with you." As God is true, that means success anywhere.

When a carpenter drives a nail, I have seen him clinch it on the other side. He said it was to prevent the nail from being pulled out. If you will clinch your experience of entire sanctification with a clear, unequivocal testimony, Satan is going to have some trouble in pulling that nail out. An experience that is driven half way in, or not clinched, works loose when the storms twist the building or the weather gets so hot that the boards warp.

THE OLD MAN.

I do not know how old the Old Man is; he was here when I came, and yet he seemed to be a very close friend, for I am told that I introduced him to my people before I could talk.

The Old Man is best pleased if you will let him go by your name. If you reject as yours some of his antics that have led you into folly he will argue that there has been a mistake all around, and prove from the leading ecclesiastics that he never did exist.

The Old Man believes in exact justice. He will fight the whole community, if necessary, to get what is coming to him.

The Old Man wants the first place in the procession. If he can wear a red sash and give orders to the parade he is happy.

The Old Man is a most elusive fellow. While at times he is very much in evidence, at other times folks will declare that he nev-

er did exist. There has been much contro-
versy also as to his name. He has been
called *primal strength,* and *human nature,*
and some have even gone so far as to give
him the bad name of sin.

The Old Man is quite sentimental, and will
use his handkerchief with much effect when
the evangelist pulls out the tremolo stop and
tells about his angel mother. To be sure, I
know that when the Old Man was a young
man his mother cut the wood and carried the
water and milked the cow, and a growl or a
muttered curse was the best praise he gave
her but "Mother, home and heaven" so stirs
up his sensibilities now, it makes him really
pious.

The Old Man really glories in a fine tem-
per. He is none of your milk and water
weaklings. He is strong, and things have to
get out of the way when he moves. In little
things about the home he may acknowledge
to nerves, if pressed, and if the law pre-
sumes to question in some case, he will admit
a brain storm.

Of course the Old Man has his faults, he
will admit that—but you had better be careful about specifying them.

The Old Man is seldom silent—unless he is
pouting. In fact he is so loquacious that he
can not always keep within the bounds of

the exact truth. But he can tell a lie and defend it with as much assurance as you can proclaim and defend the truth.

The Old Man is a great party man. His favorite boast is that he never scratched a ticket nor gave a cent to any other church than his own.

One way in which the Old Man proves his goodness and greatness is to show that nearly everybody else is bad and no account. He can tell you of hypocrites in the church by the hour; in fact, he does not just now recall a single person who does not do things he would scorn to do.

There is one thing the Old Man cannot stand, and that is for folks to know just how he really looks. He is just as good looking as you, mind you, but a little paint or powder or feathers or padding really helps him to look natural.

It will not do to say that the Old Man is proud. Not a bit of it. He is really humble. I have seen him put on old clothes, refuse to black his shoes or wear a collar, and then brag on every corner that he was not stuck up like some folks he knew.

While the Old Man is conscious of the fact that really there is no one but himself who amounts to much, he is not a solitary individual; he is gregarious. If he were to stay by himself, how could his real worth be recognized? He likes company, and so he gets some of his select fellows together and organizes a lodge, then they pass their time calling each other in turn most Exalted Ruler or Worshipful Master, or supreme Chancellor.

The Old Man dearly loves a handle to his name and will swell up when you call him "Doctor." But if he can't earn a title for himself he will hold up to scorn all who justly have them.

The Old Man has unclean eyes; you would not want to know what picture he carries in his pocket, and a city bill-board is more attractive to him than the most wonderful sunset. Yet the Old Man's strong point is in speaking evil of modest pure womanhood.

The Old Man has a fertile imagination; if he sees two friends conversing apart he can tell exactly what things they are saying about him.

The Old Man is a great braggart; when you talk about death he never mentions the subject himself. He is not afraid, but he will let the weeds grow up waist high on baby's grave before he would go into the cemetery, and lose all appetite for supper if there is a little cloud in the southwest.

The Old Man does not believe in missions. He thinks that it is a sin to send all that money to the foreign fields when we have so many heathen at home. I am suspicious that the Old Man really thinks that some of the money ought to come his way.

The Old Man sometimes has a call to preach but the brand of cigars the Bishop smokes has more interest with him than the kind of crown the martyrs wear.

The Old Man dearly loves to see his name in print, and he is going to get that kind of notoriety if even by a patent medicine testimonial.

The Old Man is quite military; he likes marching, the touch of the sword in his hand and the crowds on the sidewalk, although I have seen him pulled out from under the bed when the governor called out the militia.

The Old Man believes in religion, the right kind; but of course, he has a great contempt for superstitious tales of miracles. The supernatural is all stuff. He believes in reason but the old fellow is strong on Christian Science, Theosophy, Telepathy, Astrology, New Thought, psychic force and other such scientific religions.

The Old Man weighs not more than 175 pounds when he is at home and just can't control Billy. Billy will run off from home with bad boys that smoke, and swear, and steal; and Billy weighs all of sixty pounds.

The Old Man expects to go to heaven, of course, he does. There will be some congenial spirits there; none of these whining sanctimonious fools, they would object to a good, quiet smoke or a race story; and heaven is bound to be a place where the Old Man can enjoy himself or it wouldn't be heaven.

MUST WORK NOW.

If this is the only generation that we can reach why not every member of the Church of the Nazarene be a foreign missionary and home misionary; and a member of the Board of Education, and Church Extension; shake off all dead formality and get the scales knocked from our eyes and see the need as God sees it, and go in to succeed or die on the battle field. Here goes one of you to do his dead level best until he goes up or till Jesus comes.

In the days that you and I are living, the railroad and ship builders and mill owners and mine operators are all shouting a reduction in wages, but God thunders back from His throne and says, there is no reduction in wages. See Rom. 6:23. Hear what He says on the subject, "The wages of sin is death;

and "The soul that sinneth it shall die." "To be carnally minded is death." Oh beloved, there is no reduction in wages for Christ said, "Except ye repent, ye shall all likewise perish." So you see there is no reduction in wages. Sin carries the same penalty today that it did before the world war. Repent and live, or refuse and die and spend eternity in outer darkness away from the presence of God the Father, God the Son, and God the Holy Ghost. The old Book says, "Turn ye, turn ye, for why will ye die?'"

For the past quarter of a century many of the professors of our leading universities and also many of our leading pulpits have been telling us that Germany was fast coming to the Golden Age, and behold, about the time we looked for the gold they gave us poison gas. I wonder what the professors have up their sleeve to give us now.

NAMES FOR SANCTIFICATION.

A Hindu from India got sanctified and called it the "abundant life." John Wesley got it and called it the "second blessing." Charles Wesley got it and called it the "second rest." A beautiful old Dutch mother in Ohio got sanctified and called it running-over religion. Dr. Boardman, the great Presbyterian divine, got the blessing and called it the "rest of faith." Dr. Gordon, the great Baptist of Boston, got the blessing and called it "full assurance." St. John, the beloved Apostle, got the blessing and called it "perfect love." St. Paul got the blessing and called it "entire sanctification." When the Lord sanctified me in my cornfield I called it "the greatest thing in the world." Thank God, we were all right.

CAN'T JUDGE BY CLOTHES.

We have reached the day when you can no more judge a man in the church by the length of his coat or the height of his beautiful plug hat, for he may wear both and smell like a tobacco factory, and be an expert at riding the goat; and, it is even possible for him to sneer at the beautiful experience of entire sanctification and yet hold the highest office in the Church. His office is no evidence of his piety, his great faith in God, or his humble walk before men. What a pity that a man so small should disgrace such a high office! An office in the Church of Jesus Christ is God-appointed and God-ordained; then how dare a man come into the presence of the Almighty adorned with an Elk's head, a chopping ax, a chain link, a square and compass and letter G. Can't God see?

The experience of entire sanctification will put a fellow in touch with God and make him vote the prohibition ticket. It keeps him in harmony with heaven; it will clean out his mouth and tear the Square and Compass off of the lapel of his coat, and the letter G will disappear. He will shed off the three links. Elk's Heads can't live on the lapel of the coat of a holy soul. You will never see the Chopping Ax on the breast of a man that is wholly sanctified. Oh Beloved, this experience will put you on the side of every thing that is right and it will put you against everything that is wrong.

WHAT DOES SANCTIFICATION DO?

Well, it is the crucifixion of the Old Man; it destroys the body of sin; it does bury the Old Man face downward; it does put off the Old Man with his deeds or, in other words, the Old Man and his children. It does pull up the roots of bitterness; it is the death of the Old Adam; it is the destruction of the body of sin; it is the cleansing of the nature, the purifying of the heart of a justified believer. All of the above is the negative side of the sanctified life; the positive side is the baptism with the Holy Ghost and fire. It is the fulness of the blessing of the gospel of Christ. It is the enduement of power. It is

the promise of the Father. It is the blessing
of perfect love. It is victory over the world
and the flesh and the devil. It is now a holy
delight to live. Glory to God the Father, and
the Son, and the Holy Ghost forever and
ever, Amen. It is Jesus on the throne of
your heart and life holding the key of the
soul, spirit, and body, for now you are not
your own; you have been bought with a
price. You have handed yourself over to its
rightful owner You belong to Christ.

THROUGH THE WESTERN DESERT.

A stroll of twelve hundred miles through
the most beautiful cactus garden on earth
reaching from Los Angeles, Cal., to San Antonio, Texas. With only a few miles of
Southern California and a few miles around
El Paso, and only a few miles around San
Antonio is there much farming going on; all
the rest of that long trip is through the
western desert. But let no man say that this
desert is not one of the beautiful spots of the
earth, with the great old rugged mountains
on your left, with their old white heads
capped with snow, while off to your left a
few miles is the old Pacific Ocean with its
blue breakers rolling and tumbling over each
other, lashing the white sand shores in their
mad fury. God said thus far shall ye come

and no further, so there they stop. But O, the Cactus, the Cactus; their beauty is beyond description. While the tree is one of the most rugged that man ever put his two eyes on, no limbs and no leaves, but tens of thousands of the most dangerous looking thorns that you ever beheld. You say, "Where is their beauty?" Well reader, it is those beautiful flowers, the most beautiful colors that these eyes of mine have ever beheld. They hold you in their grip; you can't turn them loose. They are God-made. It looks like our Heavenly Father had employed the best artists of heaven, and that He had ransacked the finest paintshops of all the New Jerusalem and then mixed His colors according to the command of the God of the Universe. When the cacti bloom their blooms look like the faces of the angels, and all heaven smiles and says those colors came from our house; and nobody but an unbeliever could doubt it. Some of those rugged trees sparkled like diamonds, others looked like they were on fire; beauty surpassed beauty and glory surpassed glory. I feasted my eyes and praised the God of the Heavens. No tourist can make that trip without he doffs his hat to that garden and says God is still ahead.

GREATER LOVE TO SANCTIFY THAN JUSTIFY.

Samuel Rutherford, the saintly Scottish Presbyterian divine, said, "Christ is more to be loved for giving us sanctification than justification; it is in some respects greater love in Him to sanctify than to justify."

AN ARABIAN PROVERB.

"He who knows not, and knows not that he knows not, is a fool; avoid him. He who knows not, and knows that he knows not is simple; teach him. He who knows, and knows not that he knows is asleep; awake him. But he who knows and knows that he knows is a wise man; follow him."

The man who is sanctified wholly through the Baptism with the Holy Ghost and fire, is not of the think-so, guess-so, hope-so, trust-so, crowd, but belongs to the know-so band who have gone through to rock bottom, and with the whole armor of God on are going through with Jesus.

John Wesley said, "I dare no more fret than I dare curse and swear." He was surely a very wise man. How different nowadays; the average man in the Church is fretting his poor life away. I judge that several thousand people have taken me to one side in the past forty years of my ministry and reproved me for laughing when I preach;

but to a man and a woman, they looked sad
and despondent, disappointed and disrupted,
and had become chronic fault-finders. O beloved, if God fills your soul with His love He
is liable to put some laughter in your mouth.

Some one has said, "On every faded leaf
of your scrap--book, on that pile of faded
flowers, on that little empty crib and the vacant chair, the little folded dress, the little
shoes in the tray of the trunk, and that little
green mound on the hill side, was written,
God is love. Then somebody wrote that
beautiful old hymn, "We will understand it
better by and by."   Even so, Amen.

If a man therefore purge himself from
these, he shall be a vessel unto honor, sanctified, and meet for the Master's use, and
prepared unto every good work."   Let's read
this verse again and see how it reads. "If a
man therefore purge himself from these, he
shall be a vessel unto honor." If a man
therefore purge himself from these, he shall
be sanctified. If a man therefore purge
himself from these, he shall be meet for the
Master's use. If a man therefore purge
himself from these, he shall be prepared unto every good work. Let's read this verse
again and see how it reads. If a man therefore will not purge himself from these, he
will not be sanctified. If a man therefore

will not purge himself from these, he will not be meet for the Master's use. If a man therefore will not purge himself from these, he will not be prepared unto every good work. See 2 Tim. 2:21.

In the 119th Psalm and the 73rd verse we have a gold nugget! "Thy hands have made me and fashioned me: give me understanding, that I may learn thy commandments.'"

"But thou hast fully known my doctrine, manner of life, purpose, faith, longsuffering, charity, patience, persecutions, afflictions, which came unto me at Antioch, at Iconium, at Lystra; what persecutions I endured; but out of them all the Lord delivered me." 2 Tim. 3:10, 11. What a record this man made. He lived like a martyr, he could die the death of a hero. He walked the earth an uncrowned king. He had grace enough to be a saint; he had wisdom enough to be wise; he had humility enough to be humble; he lost his head but God made the world take it up and crown it, for he stands out in a class by himself for real down-right manhood.

One of the most remarkable things about the Bible is this; that often such a short word opens up such a long subject. Take this wonderful statement—be ye holy. 1 Pet. 1:15.

Be filled with the Spirit. Eph. 5:18. Be witnesses. Acts 1:8. Be faithful. Rev. 2:10. Be honest. Rom. 12:17. Be patient toward all men. 1 Thess. 5:14. Be of good comfort. 2nd Cor. 13:11. Be perfect. 2nd Cor. 13:11. Be of one mind. 2nd Cor. 13:11. Be not overcome of evil, but overcome evil with good. Rom. 12:21. Be without dissimulation. Rom. 12:9. Be kindly affectioned one to another. Rom. 12:10. Be of the same mind one toward another. Rom. 12:16. Be not unequally yoked together with unbelievers. 2nd Cor. 6:14. Be ye angry and sin not. Eph. 4:26. Be not ye therefore partakers with them. Eph. 5:7. Be careful for nothing. Phil. 4:6. Be rich in good works. 1st Tim. 6:18. Be not thou therefore ashamed of the testimony of our Lord. 2nd Tim. 1:8. Be thou an example of the believers. 1st Tim. 4:12. Be teachers. Heb. 5:12. Be of good courage. Psa. 31:24. Be ye doers of the word. James 1:22. Be ye religious. James 1:26. Be not many masters. James 3:1. Be afflicted and mourn and weep. James 4:9. Be followers of that which is good. 1st Peter 3:13. Be ye therefore sober and watch unto prayer. 1st Peter 4:7. Be reproached for the name of Christ. 1st Peter 4:14. Be sober, be vigilant, because your adversary the devil as a roaring lion, walketh about seeking whom he may devour. 1st Peter 5:8.

The reader will see by this time that my bees have swarmed, and these beautiful quotations are just a sample of what we find in the blessed old Book. How rich is the man that owns a Bible and reads it and believes it. His fortune is absolutely made. I don't wonder that King David said, Thy word is a lamp unto my feet, and a light unto my pathway." I am not surprised that he said, "Thy word have I hid in mine heart, that I might not sin against thee."

DURING THE YEAR 1922.

I don't want my chunk fire to ever be found twice in the same settlement. I want to move on to a better country. I want to make tracks and lay fast patters. I want to believe more, walk closer, live higher, dig deeper, and climb more of the great mountains of difficulties and overcome more obstacles, and cut a swath through more surrounding circumstances. I want to stand straighter, run faster, jump higher, wabble less than during any year of my Christian experience. Remember there is nothing so beautiful as grace, and nothing so hateful as sin. Nothing so uplifting as righteousness, and nothing so destructive as wicked-

ness. You must make your choice. It is up
to you to make good or make bad. Don't
forget that God said to the saint, "Many are
the afflictions of the righteous but the Lord
delivereth him out of them all." Don't forget
that God said to the sinner, "Be sure your
sin will find you out."

There is nothing so beautiful in the home
as a great flock of children, and nothing so
disappointing as to see a home childless.
There is nothing so disgusting as to see a
woman leading down the street a dog with a
blue ribbon on his neck. The idea of as
great a thing as woman trying to set her affections on a dog. It is a delusion of the
devil. She is not a happy woman. She is
miserable, and wretched, and poor, and
naked, and blind. God created woman for
motherhood, and it is absolutely impossible
for a woman to disobey the command of God
and try to make up for her misfortune by
setting her affections on a dog or a tom-cat.
It can't be done. It never has been done, and
it never will be done. I make a public con-
fession right here. It takes all the grace
that I can pull down to keep me from back-
sliding when I meet a woman on the streets
of our cities leading a pug nose bull-dog with
a brass collar on.

THE DAWN OF DAY.

In the songs of King Solomon, 6:10, we read, "Who is she that looketh forth as the morning, fair as the moon, clear as the sun, and terrible as an army with banners." This beautiful text is said to be a description of the Church of our Lord and Savior Jesus Christ. The reader will see that all the marks of a great and glorious Church are brought out in the text. The word "she" denotes motherhood. It takes the mother to give life. We read again that, "When Zion travails she brings forth sons and daughters." Notice again, "She looketh forth." There is expectation and desire on the part of the mother. The whole clause says that "She looketh forth as the morning." There is something about the morning that can't be described by man; it is absolutely impossible. Who can picture the early morning? Thank God we never tire of the morning; it is always fresh and invigorating, and we would like it to last all day. See the dewdrops on the grass; see the honey bees out after their morning meal; hear them hum; just listen to the bleating of the lambs, see them hop and skip and leap over the old stump in the meadow. My! my! listen to the calves as they bawl and kick up their heels and gallop across the pasture; and the old

turkey is gobbling to beat himself, and the
roosters are crowing themselves hoarse on
the barnyard fence; the mocking-bird has
just tuned up his little throat, and just list-
en to him as he plays his horn one minute,
and his flute the next. Man, that music was
inspired by the Lord Himself. Now the old
Bob White on that fencing post is letting
the whole settlement know that he is up in
time for business; and a half dozen gray
squirrels are up one hickory tree barking
like they owned the whole place. We wonder what all of this frolicking is going on
about and the answer comes back that this is
the breaking of the day; this is the morning,
and all nature rejoices to see the sun rise.

There is nothing on the face of the earth
like it. This is a fact; when the sun shuts
his eyes behind the western skies all nature
goes to slumbering, but when he opens his
eyes in the eastern skies all nature meets
him laughing. See that baby boy in that
crib, as he laughs and crows and plays with
his toes. His little mother is in the back yard
hanging out the clothes. He just seems to
own the whole ranch. Listen to him whoop!
What ails him; well, this is the morning.
As he lieth there and shakes in his fat and
chuckles he makes you think of the sunshine
and the dewdrops on the honeysuckle vines;

nothing old and stale there. All nature is shouting with that baby boy. That is just a life-sized photo of the Church of Jesus Christ.

FAIR AS THE MOON.

The next clause says that she is as "fair as the moon." The great men of the earth have said many beautiful things about the moon, but she is better looking than they said she was. She is like a young man's sweetheart; there is something about the moon that naturally suggests a courtship. There have been more matches made by moonshine than was ever made by sunshine, or even candlelight. A young man with a pretty maiden on his arm strolling down the beautiful old country road toward the old-fashioned country church, with the pale moonshine glimmering on their pathway, can hardly keep from getting up a courtship. It is natural and beautiful, and God-ordained. So in this beautiful picture we have the bride of Christ compared to the moon. "As *fair* as the *moon*" is the wording of it. The moon seems to set out there somewhere on the hills of glory dressed up in her silver gown and the stars seem to bloom out on every hill and mountain top of the glory world. O beloved, a greater than John the Baptist has been at work out there. Just

90 NUGGETS OF GOLD

watch that moon rise and shake down her
silver rays on this little country of ours.
She is the blushing maid of that upper world
and all men adore her. They just have it to
do. They can't help themselves.

CLEAR AS THE SUN.

We see again that the next picture of the
Church is that she is as "clear as the sun."
The sun is the hope of the world. There is
no vegetable life without sunshine, and
there could be no animal life without it. So
beloved, we must have sunshine or we will
have to give up life and take to a hole in the
ground. There is no spiritual life without
the Church. We must look to the Church of
Jesus Christ to furnish this old world with
spiritual life. I know that sometimes it
looks like the Church had married the world
and that their children die before they are
born, but this is not always the case. Thank
God, sometimes the revival spirit strikes the
country and the old Mother Church rises up
in her beauty and grandeur and you hear the
children shouting and you know that Zion
has been travailing and that sons and daughters have been born into the kingdom of the
Lord Jesus Christ. All heaven goes to re-
joicing in the fact, that Zion has been bringing forth sons and daughters.

AN ARMY WITH BANNERS.

The next statement we have of the Church that she is as "Terrible as an army with banners." It has been said that in olden times that when an army started out to conquer a country that every battle that they won that they were given a banner, and if they won enough battles that every soldier carried a banner. Don't you see that if such an army was to come to a city and every soldier had a banner that it meant that they had conquered every army that they had met and the city at once would simply throw up her hands and surrender without firing a gun. That is a picture of the Church of Jesus Christ, Don't you see that if every Church member carried a banner with his soul on fire for God, and with glory all over his face, that the sinners of the country would fall down before such an army and beg for mercy and, thank God, find it and join the army at once and go to waving his banner as he marched from this old world to glory.

THE HOLY SPIRIT DISPENSATION.

We read that back in the Old Testament under the dispensation of the Father, that at times the Holy Spirit was said to come on men, and when he came upon them they did exploits.

We also read that during the days of the blessed Christ, and under His dispensation, that the Holy Spirit was with his disciples. We find that statement throughout the New Testament.

Again we read that under the dispensation of the Holy Ghost he was to be in the saints, and dwell in them; so we see the three dispensations and how the Holy Spirit worked in each. In the first, He came on men at times; in the second, He was with the children of God; and in the third, He was to dwell *within* them.

Without a doubt in my mind the longest and straightest road that has ever been built was built by our gracious heavenly Father, and it is called the "Path of life.'

The most prolific tree that has ever been heard of is without a doubt the one that is described in the 22 Chapter of Rev., and the 2nd verse. We read there of a tree that bore twelve manner of fruit and yielded her fruit every month. Also the leaves of the tree were for the healing of the nations. This remarkable tree is called the "Tree of Life." In the 14th verse we read, "Blessed are they that do His commandments, that they may have right to the tree of life."

In studying Bible Geography we find out the highest mountain in the world is not located on this side of the blue breakers, but it is described in the blessed old Book as Mount Zion. From the top of this mountain we have good view of Heaven, Glory to Jesus!

Again, we find by studying Bible Geography that the longest River in the world is the river of life. The river of life is so long that she makes the Old Miss ashamed of herself.

When I took my first lesson in Bible Geology I discovered the Rock of Ages and built a house on it, and the Devil has never been able to turn it over or even knock out a window, and the roof hasn't leaked in 42 years. Glory to God!

While taking a beautiful lesson one day in Bible Botany the blessed Christ came along and plucked from the Rose of Sharon and the Lily of the Valley a most beautiful bouquet and pinned it on the lapel of my soul. It almost perfumed the whole settlement and every time that I got a glimpse of my flowers I had a shouting spell.

While studying Bible Astronmy some forty-two years ago, I discovered the Morning Star, and thank God, it lifted me above the fog and mist of this old world and put such an eternal go-through in my soul that

Jupiter and Venus have looked very small to me ever since, and I have been able to sing with Charles Wesley,

"I rode on the sky, freely justified I,
  Nor did envy Elijah his seat;
My soul mounted higher in a chariot of
    fire,
  And the moon it was under my feet."

Apart from the Bible I have never read a book on Biology, but while studying that blessed old Book one day, to my glad surprise I discovered the Lion of the Tribe of Judah, and bless your heart and life, He broke every fetter from my heart and set me free; "put a new song in my mouth, even praises unto our God." We read, "In him was life, and the life was the light of men, and he that followeth him shall not walk in darkness but shall have the light of life."

WHEN FATHER RODE THE GOAT.

The house is full of arnica,
  And mystery profound;
We do not dare to run about,
  Or make the slightest sound;
We leave the big piano shut
  And do not strike a note;
The doctor's been here seven times
  Since Father rode the goat.

He joined a lodge a week ago,
   Got in at 4 A. M.,
And sixteen brethren brought him home,
   Though he says he brought them;
His wrist was sprained and one big rip
   Had rent his Sunday coat;
There must have been a lively time
   When Father rode the goat.

He's resting on the couch today
   And practicing the signs—
The hailing sign, the working grip,
   And other monkey shines;
He mutters pass words 'neath his breath,
   And other things he'll quote;
They surely had an evening's work
   When Father rode the goat.

This goat leads, what Teddy calls,
   A very strenuous life,
Makes trouble for such candidates
   As tickle him in strife;
But somehow when we mention it,
   Pa wears a look so grim,
We wonder if he rode the goat,
   Or if the goat rode him.
              —*By C. H. Reynolds,*
          The Railroad Telegrapher.

A good motto to hang on the pulpit when
you are having a testimony meeting is simp-

ly this; have a motto made from white oilcloth about eighteen inches wide and probably two feet long and have the painting in large letters of black and red and blue, as follows:

"My trouble is talking too long. I will cut off both ends and put fire in the middle."

I learned a beautiful old song some 45 years ago, when I was a boy. It was called "My Grandfather's Clock." Since then the Rev. Arthur E. Lewis has made immortal a beautiful hymn on the doctrine and experience of sanctification, and has set the words to the music of the song. The original words were as follows:

MY GRANDFATHER'S CLOCK.

My Grandfather"s clock was too large for
    the shelf,
  So it stood ninety years on the floor;
It was taller by half than the old man himself,
  Though it weighed not a pennyweight
    more;
It was bought on the morn of the day that he
    was born,
  And was always his treasure and his pride,
But it stopped short, never to go again,
  When the old man died.

CHORUS.

Ninety years without slumbering, tick, tick,
    tick, tick!
His life seconds numbering, tick, tick, tick,
    tick!
But it stopped short, never to go again,
When the old man died.

In watching the pendulum swing to and fro,
    Many hours had he spent when a boy,
In childhood and manhood the clock seemed
        to know
    And to share both his grief and his joy;
For it struck twenty-four as he enter the
        door
    With his blooming and beautiful bride,
But it stopped short, never to go again,
    When the old man died.

My Grandfather said that of those that he
        could hire,
    Not a servant so faithful he found,
For it wasted not time and it had but one
        design,
    At the close of the week to be wound;
For it kept in its place not a frown upon its
        face,
    Nor its hands ever hung by its side,
But it stopped short, never to go again,
    When the old man died.

THE HOOSIER POET.

Have yer heard ther Hoosier poet,
  Ther feller what writ them farm song?
Well, when yer trav'lin' on ther train,
  Jist the thing fer to take along.

When yer wants to know poetry,
  Jist put in yer time readin' that;
Make yer wish yer was back agin,
  Sittin' under yer old straw hat.

Make yer wish yer was goin' fishin',
  With yer line and old hick'ry pole,
Make yer think how yer pulled 'em out,
  Sittin' thar by the swimmin' hole.

My! how the times has changed since then,
  And the old friends are far away,
They sleep 'neath the shade of the trees,
  Till the dawn of a brighter day.
                    —*J. P. Coleman.*

WHY WE PREACH HOLINESS.

Some good people have wondered why we were so dull as to preach Scriptural Holiness. Well, here are just a few of the reasons:

1st, Because God the Father is holy. 1st Peter 1:15.

2nd, Because Christ is Holy. Luke 1:35.

3rd, Because God's Spirit is a Holy Spirit,

and His office work is to make men holy. Rom. 15:16.

4th, Because the angels are holy. Matt. 25:31.

5th, Because heaven is a holy place. Rev. 21:10.

6th, Because the Bible is a holy Book. 2 Tim. 3:16, 17.

7th, Because God's commands are holy. Rom. 7:12.

8th, Because God's law is holy. Rom. 7:12.

9th, Because God's preachers and bishops are to be holy. Titus 1:7, 8.

10th, Because God's prophets are holy. 2 Peter 1:21.

11th, Because God's Apostles were holy. Eph. 3:5.

12th, Because the brethren are holy. 1 Thess. 5:27.

13th, Because God's women were holy. 1 Peter 3:5.

14th, Because it is God's will. 1 Thess. 4:3.

15th, Because God calls us to it. 1 Thess. 4:7.

16th, Because God chose us unto holiness. Eph. 1:4.

17th, Because God chastises His people to bring them to holiness. Heb. 12:10.

18th, Because Christ died that we might be made holy. Heb. 13:12.

19th, Because the Holy Ghost witnesses to it. Heb. 10:14, 15, 16.

20th, Because God is not ashamed of us when we have got it. Heb. 2:11.

21st, Because we can't see God without it. Heb. 12:14.

22nd, Because it was promised us. Luke 24:49.

23rd, Because it is our inheritance. Acts 20:31.

24th, Because God commanded us to be holy. 1 Peter 1:16.

25th, Because God said that we were to live holy all the days of our lives, and that doesn't mean the last days of our lives. Luke 1:73, 74.

27th, Because God the Father sanctifies us. Jude 1:1.

28th, Because Christ sanctifies us. Eph. 5:25, 26, 27.

29th, Because the Holy Ghost sanctifies us. Rom. 15:16.

30th, Because it makes God's people one. St. John 17:21.

31st, Because it makes God and His people one. Heb. 2:11.

32nd, Because the world will believe when they see you sanctified. St. John 17:21.

33rd, Because the heathen shall know. Ezekiel 36:23.

34th, Because St. Paul professed holiness. 1 Thess. 2:10.

35th, Because St. Paul professed Christian Perfection.   Phil. 3:15.

36th, Because Peter and John professed it. Acts 3:12.

37th, Because the holy brethren were partakers of the heavenly calling.   Heb. 3:1.

38th, Because the Epistle to the Thessalonians was to be read to all the holy brethren.   1 Thess. 5:27.

39th, Because the holy are to have part in the first resurrection.   Rev. 20:6.

40th, Because Enoch walked with God 300 years and was taken to heaven alive.   Gen. 5:22, 23, 24.   Do you think he was holy?

41st, Because God commanded Abraham to walk before him and be perfect. Gen. 17:1.

42nd, Because we are to walk before God and be perfect.   Deut. 18:13.

43rd, Because he that is holy is to be holy still.   Rev. 22:11.

44th, Because Elijah went to heaven alive. Do you think he could get in without it? Rev. 21:27.

45th, Because Elisha was a holy man.   2 Kings 4:9.

46th, Because Noah was a holy man. Gen. 6:9,

47th, Because we are to put off the old leaven. 1 Cor. 5:6, 7.

48th, Because we are to crucify the Old Man. Rom. 6:6.

49th, Because we are to put off the Old Man. Eph. 4:22.

50th, Because we have put off the Old Man. Col. 3:9.

51st, Because we are created in righteousness and true holiness. Eph. 4:24.

If the reader wants any more Book I have plenty left.

DON'TS FOR CHURCH-GOERS.

Don't visit. Worship.

Don't hurry away. Speak and be spoken to.

Don't stop in the end of the pew. Move over.

Don't monopolize your hymn-book. Be neighborly.

Don't wait for introductions. Introduce yourself.

Don't choose the back seat. Leave it for late comers.

Don't dodge the collection plate. Pay what you are able.

Don't criticise. Remember, and think on your own frailties.

Don't stare blankly while others sing, read, pray. Join in.

Don't leave without praying God's blessing upon all present.

Don't sit while others stand or kneel. Share in the service.

Don't sit with your hand to your head as if worshiping hurt you.

Don't dodge the preacher. Show yourself friendly.   *—James G. Tucker,*
in the Central Christian Advocate.

AT CHURCH NEXT SUNDAY.

If I knew you and you knew me,
How little trouble there would be.
We pass each other on the street,
But just come out and let us meet,
    At church next Sunday.

Each one intends to do what's fair,
And treat his neighbor on the square,
But he may not quite understand
Why you don't take him by the hand
    At church next Sunday.

This world is sure a busy place,
And we must hustle in the race.
For social hours some are not free
The six week days, but all should be
    At church next Sunday.

We have an interest in our town,
The dear old place must not go down;
We want to push good things along.
And we can help some if we're strong
    At church next Sunday.

Don't knock and kick and slam and slap
At everybody on the map,
But push and pull and boost and boom,
And use up all the standing room
    At church next Sunday.

                —Anon.

IN MEMORIAM.

A precious one from us is gone,
  A voice we love is stilled,
A place is vacant in our home,
  Which never can be filled.

'Tis hard to break the tender chord,
  Where love has bound the heart,
'Tis hard. so hard to speak the words,
  "We must forever part."

Yet again we hope to meet them,
  When the day of life is fled,
And in heaven with joy to greet them,
  Where no farewell tears are shed.

She is safe in the arms of Jesus,
  Safe on His gentle breast,
There by His love o'er shaded
  Sweetly her soul is at rest.

God in His heavenly wisdom
  Has claimed the boon His love had given,
And though the body molders here
  The soul is safe in heaven.
                —*Mrs. R. E. Fletcher.*

KERNELS OF TRUTH.

"To be anxious for souls and yet not impatient, to be patient and not indifferent, to bear the infirmities of the weak without fostering them, to testify against sin, and unfaithfulness, and the low standard of spiritual life and yet to keep the stream of love free and full and open, to have the mind of a faithful loving shepherd, a hopeful physician, a tender nurse, skilful teacher, requires the continual renewal of the Lord's Grace."

I must have another day; not for repentance, not for getting right with God—this day has been ample for that—but for work. I come to sunset with so many things undone, and yet I have just begun to learn how.

Gold is powerful—some say all powerful—in this city of Time, but of the cities of Eternity, toward which we journey, but one door can be opened with the key of gold—and that, the gates of darkness and despair.

The heavier the church is in the kitchen the lighter it is in the prayer meeting. The

church that goes in for entertainment has no
time for regeneration and sanctification.

God's love calls for fellowship, and his service for mutuality. If God's service is a
weariness to you, your service to God is a
weariness to Him.

It is easier to hang on, than to put in. The
less of spirituality we have within, the more
of other things we seek to put on the outside.
When glory departs, formality comes in.
Machinery is the world's substitute for the
Holy Ghost.

HOW PRAYER WAS ANSWERED.

"Madam, we miss the train at B——."
  "But can't you make it, sir?" she gasped?
"Impossible; it leaves at three,
  And we are due a quarter past."
"Is there no way? Oh, tell me, then,
  Are you a Christian?" "I am not."
"And are there none among the men
  Who run the train?" "No—I forgot—
I think this fellow over here,
  Oiling the engine, claims to be."
She threw upon the engineer
  A fair face white with agony.

"Are you a Christian?" "Yes, I am."
  "Then, oh, sir, won't you pray with me,
All the long way, that God will stay,
  That God will hold the train at B——?"

"'Twill do not good; it's due at three,
And"—"Yes, but God can hold the train;
   My dying child is calling me,
   And I must see her face again.
Oh, won't you pray?" "I will," a nod
   Emphatic as he takes his place.
When Christians grasp the arm of God
They grasp the power that rules the rod.

Out from the station swept the train,
   On time, swept on past wood and lea;
The engineer, with cheeks aflame,
   Prayed, "O Lord, hold the train at B——,"
Then flung the throttle wide, and like
   Some giant monster of the plain,
With panting sides and mighty strides,
   Past hill and valley swept the train.

A half, a minute, two are gained;
   Along those burnished lines of steel,
His glances leap, each nerve is strained,
   And still he prays with fervent zeal.
Heart, hand and brain, with one accord,
   Work while his pray'r ascends to heaven.
"Just hold the train eight minutes, Lord,
   And I'll make up the other seven."

With rush and roar through meadow lands,
   Past cottage homes and green hillsides,
The panting thing obeys his hands,
   And speeds along with giant strides.

They say an accident delayed
  The train a little while; but He
Who listened while His children prayed,
  In answer, held the train at B———.
                 —*Sel.*

SLAP HIM ON THE BACK.

James Whitcomb Riley

If you should meet a fellow-man with trou-
    ble's flag unfurled,
  And lookin' like he didn't have a friend in
    all the world,
Go up and slap him on the back, and holler,
    "How d' you do?"
  And grasp his hand so warm he'll know he
    has a friend in you.

Then ask what's hurtin' him, and laugh his
    cares away,
  And tell him that the darkest night is just
    before the day.
Don't talk in graveyard palaver, but say it
    right out loud
  That God will sprinkle sunshine in the
    trail of every cloud.

This world at best is but a hash of pleasure
    and of pain,—
  Some days are bright and sunny, and some
    all splashed with rain,

And that's just how it ought to be, for when
 the clouds roll by
We'll know just how to 'preciate the bright
 and smiling sky.

So learn to take it as it comes, and don't
 sweat at the pores
Because the Lord's opinion doesn't coin-
 cide with yours;
But always keep rememberin', when cares
 your path enshroud,
That God has lots of sunshine to spill behind the cloud.

A LORD'S PRAYER CURIOSITY.

The following is one of the most remarkable compositions ever written. It evinces an
ingenuity peculiarly its own. The initial letters spell, "My boast is in the glorious cross
of Christ." The words in capitals, when
read on the left-hand side from top to bottom, and on the right-hand side from bottom
to top, form the Lord's Prayer complete:—

Make known the Gospel truth, OUR Father
 King;
Yield up Thy Grace, dear FATHER from
 above;
Bless us with hearts WHICH feelingly can
 sing—

"Our life Thou ART for EVER, God of
     Love."
Assuage our grief IN love FOR Christ we
     pray,
Since the Prince of HEAVEN and GLORY
     died,
Took all sins and HALLOWED THE display.
Infinte BEing, first man, AND then was
     crucified.
Stupendous God! THY grace and POWER
     make known;
In Jesus' NAME let all THE world rejoice.
Now labour in THY Heavenly KINGDOM
     own,
That blessed KINGDOM, for Thy saints
     THE choice,
How vile to COME to Thee IS all our cry;
Enemies to THYself and all that's THINE!
Graceless our WILL we live FOR vanity;
Loathing the very BEing, EVIL in design—
O God, Thy will be DONE FROM earth to
     heaven;
Reclining ON the Gospel let US live,
In EARTH from sin, DELIVERed and for-
     given.
Oh! AS Thyself, BUT teach us to forgive;
Unless ITs power TEMPTATION doth de-
     stroy.
Sure IS our fall INTO the depths of woe.
Carnal IN mind, we have NOT a glimpse of
     joy

Raised against HEAVEN; in US no hope we know.

Oh, GIVE us grace AND LEAD us on the way;

Shine on US with Thy Love, and give US peace.

Self, and THIS sin that rises AGAINST us, slay.

Oh, grant each DAY our TRESPASSes may cease,

Forgive OUR evil deeds, THAT oft we do;

Convince us DAILY of THEM, to our shame;

Help us with Heavenly BREAD, FORGIVE us, too,

Recurrent lusts; AND WE'll adore Thy name,

In Thy FORGIVEness we AS saints can die,

Since for US and our TRESPASSES so high,

Thy Son, OUR Saviour died on Calvary.

W. R., Chance Inn, Ceres, Fife.

IN THE GOOD OLD FASHIONED WAY.

By F. M. Lehman.

Often my mother used to tell me in the days of long ago, that our race had deeply fallen by a strong and wily foe. Oft she told me that old Satan came to Eden in disguise, thus deceiving Eve and Adam by a chain of subtle lies. Then she taught me that the

angel drove them from the Garden fair; that
our race was doomed to perish in an utter-
most despair. Then she took her dear old
Bible from the table at her side; read to me
the wondrous story of the Savior crucified;
how He died by all forsaken on old Calvary's
rugged tree that the race might have redemption and be made forever free. O, this
set my heart atremble, for she told the story
well—how our Christ had died to save us
from an everlasting Hell. And though
thoughtless, wild and sinful through the
years of yesterday, yet I know my mother
served Him in the good old fashioned way.

And how often mother lingered with her
hand upon my head; praying that the Lord
would save me, as I sought my trundle bed.
As the golden moonbeams fell there in great
patches on the floor, I just promised God and
mother that I'd live in sin no more. O, how
sweet those days of childhood when His
grace first touched me there; when my sins
were all forgiven; birds were singing everywhere. Though I wandered far from mother, father, home, and Heaven and God, till
I felt the bitter sin-stings; bowed beneath
the chastening rod; yet the memory of my
childhood would so oft come back to me, that
I wept in silent anguish, all my soul in agony. Seemed I heard my father praying;

heard my mother's pleading tone, calling, calling for the wanderer, drifting, drifting far from Home. But at last the music of those prayers from out the yesterday brought me back to home and Jesus and the good old fashioned way.

The story mother told me of the Savior crucified, is scoffed at by the skeptic; by some scholars(?) is denied. They say there was no Jonah, and, of course, there was no whale; that it is wrong to preach a Hell that makes the sinner quail. "Salvation's universal," say these twentieth century men; they try to prove it by the stars and by their "modern pen." They laugh at our revivals, and the holiness we preach; denounce a bench for mourners, and the way we converts teach. They say there's no atonement; that we have no carnal trait; that sin is a misnomer—all will make the Golden Gate! But all this modern twaddle from the school of "modern thought" in the great white light of Judgment will but sadly come to naught. I will cling to mother's story, told me in life's yesterday, and go all the way with Jesus in the good old fashioned way.

See! the brush of Time is tracing lines and furrows on my brow; and the crimson jet of childhood throbs in feebler pulsebeats now. Soon I'll reach that moment where the silver cord shall loose and fall; sleep the sleep that knows no waking till the resurrection call. Then in Glory with the angels, Jesus, and the ransomed throng, I shall tune my silver harp-strings to the great immortal song sung by all the choirs of Heaven; by the blood-redeemed host, praising, praising, praising ever, Father, Son and Holy Ghost! Mother, father; brother, sister; wife and children, gone before, will be there to greet my coming on that ever changeless Shore; and my soul, in very rapture, will break forth in glad acclaim, shouting glory! glory ever! glory! glory to His name! Brother, sister! O, be faithful! soon will come the crowning day when we'll praise the Lord forever for the good old fashioned way!

THE LORD'S PRAYER.

The following beautiful composition was captured during the war at Charleston, S. C. It was printed on heavy satin, July 4, 1823. It was picked up by A. P. Green, of Auburn, Ind., at Corinth, Miss., the morning the Confederate forces evacuated it, May 30th, 1862.

Thou to the mercy-seat our souls doth gath-
     er,
To do our duty unto Thee, *Our Father.*
To whom all praise, all honor should be giv-
     en;

For thou art the great God *who art in heav-
    en..*
Thou by Thy wisdom, rul'st the world's
    whole frame;
Forever, therefore, *Hallowed be thy name;*
Let never more delay divide us from
Thy glorious grace, but let *Thy Kingdom
    come;*
Let thy commands opposed be by none;
But Thy good pleasure and *Thy will be done,*
And let our promptness to obey, be even
The very same *On earth as 'tis in heaven,*
Then for our souls, O, Lord, we also pray,
Thou would'st be please to *Give us. this day,*
The food of life, wherewith our souls are fed
Sufficient raiment and *Our daily bread,*
With every needful thing do thou relieve us,
And of Thy mercy, pity *And forgive us*
All our misdeeds for Him whom Thou did'st
    please
To make an offering for *Our Trespasses,*
And forasmuch, O Lord, as we believe
That thou will pardon us *As we forgive,*
Let that love teach, wherewith Thou dost ac-
    quaint us, to
Pardon all *Those who Trespass against us,*
And though sometimes thou find'st we have
    forgot,
This love for Thee, yet help *And lead us not.*
Through soul or body's want or desperation,

Nor let earth's gain drive us *Into Temptation*
Let not the soul of any true believer
Fail in the time of trial, *but deliver,*
Yea, save them from the malice of the devil,
And both in life and death, keep *Us from evil*
Thus pray we, Lord, for that of Thee, from whom
This may be had *For thine is the Kingdom,*
This world is of Thy work, its wondrous story,
To thee belongs *The power and the glory,*
And all thy wondrous works have ended never,
But will remain forever and *Forever,*
Thus we poor creatures would confess again,
And thus would say eternally *Amen.*

HELL.

E. A. Fergerson.

WHAT IS IT?

1. A lake of fire. Rev. xx, 15.
2. A bottomless pit. Rev. xx, 1.
3. A horrible tempest. Ps. xi, 6.
4. Everlasting burnings. Isa. xxxiii, 14.
5. A furnace of fire. Matt. xiii, 41-42.
6. Everlasting destruction. 2 Thess. i, 9.
7. A devouring fire. Isa. xxxiii, 14.
8. A place of torments. Luke xvi, 23.
9. A place of everlasting punishment. Matt. xxv, 46.

10. A place where people pray. Luke xvi, 27.

11. A place where they scream for mercy.. Luke xvi, 24.

12. A place where they wail. Matt. xxxiii, 42.

14. A place where they can NEVER repent. Matt. xii, 32.

15. A place of filthiness. Rev. xxii, 10-11.

16. A place of weeping. Matt. viii, 12.

17. A place of sorrows. Psa. xviii, 5.

18. A place of outer darkness. Matt. viii, 12.

19. A place where they have no rest. Rev. 14, 11.

20. A place that has gates. Matt. xvi, 18.

21. A place where they gnaw their tongues. Rev. xvi, 10.

22. A place where sores are on their bodies. Rev. xvi, 11.

23. A place of blackness and darkness forever. Jude 13.

24. A place where their worm dieth not Mark ix, 48.

25. A place where the fire is not quencher. Mark ix, 48.

26. A place where the whole body is cast. Matt. xxiv, 30.

27. A place where they will be tormented with fire. Luke xvi, 24.

28. A place where they will be tormented with brimstone. Rev. xiv, 10.

29. A place where they will burn like lime. Isa. xxxiii, 12.

30. A place where they will drink the wine of the wrath of God. Rev. xiv, 10.

31. A place where they do not want their loved ones to come. Luke xvi, 28.

32. A place where their breath will be a living flame. Isa. xxxiii, 11.

33. A place prepared for the devil and his angels. Matt. xxv, 41.

34. A place where they scream for one drop of water. Luke xvi, 24.

35. A place where there are dogs and sorcerers and whoremongers. Rev. xxii, 15.

36. A place where there are murderers, and liars, fearful and abominable. Rev. xxi, 8.

37. A storm of burning coals of fire. Ps. xi, 6. (margin).

38. Alake of fire into which people are cast alive. Rev. xix, 20.

39. A place where their torment ascendeth up forever and forever. Rev. xiv, 11.

40. A place of damnation world without end. Mark iii, 29.

POOR, BUT RICH.

A poor, blind woman in Paris, we are told, put twenty-seven francs into a plate at a missionary meeting.

"You cannot afford so much," said one.

"Yes, sir, I can," she answered.

On being pressed to explain, she said: "I am blind, and I said to my fellow straw workers: 'How much money do you spend in a year for oil in your lamps when it is too dark to work nights?' They replied 'Twenty-seven francs.'

"So," said the poor woman, "I found that I have saved so much in the year because I am blind and do not need a lamp, and I give it to shed light in heathen lands."

Every rose has its thorn, every sweet its bitter. The blacker the storm cloud, the more intensely bright the chain of fire stretched across its bosom. The darker the night, the brighter the days. After all, the shadows may be the price we pay for our sunshine. I have sometimes wondered if sorrow is not only just the interest on all the joy God has given us.—*Exchange.*

NUGGETS.

The bishops said there was something "radically wrong," but the tobacco smoke was so thick the church failed to find it.

I often find strength when I cease to struggle.

Brother, don't whine that the devil is after you. Thank God for that, and keep making tracks for glory.

When the preacher steps on my toes, I cry out, "O! how dare you hurt my neighbor so?"

You "hope so, but wish you KNEW." Beloved, for a few cents you can get a certified copy of the title deeds, giving the location of your eternal home, and a clear description of the way to reach it.

Sorrow is often God's spade that He uses to dig deeper foundation for our joy.

If "Jordan is a hard road to travel," suppose you remove some of the stones out of the way of the next fellow.

Sunshine within will make the underside of the clouds look rosy.

Don't get discouraged and run because that lick you gave the devil didn't kill him. Up! and thank God for the privilege of hitting him again.

Jesus knows our secret sins.

HIGH LICENSE.

"A thousand dollar license," said the man
    behind the bar,

As he lightly knocked the ashes from his No.
    1 cigar ;

"Well, I guess that I can stand it if the other
    fellow can,

But I'll have to shape my business on the
    thousand dollar plan,

And if the law insists on the thousand dollar
    raid,

I will have to shift the burden to the should-
    ers of my trade—

Or, rather, to the stomachs, if their stomachs
    can sustain,

And their kidneys stand the pressure of this
    thousand dollar strain.

And I'll drown them and I'll drench them,
    and I'll do my level best,

Till the dear old oaken bucket sighs for soli-
    tude and rest;

And I'll mix them, and I'll fix them with the
    cheapest, vilest stuff,

Till the kidneys holler 'murder' and the liver
    shouts 'enough.'

And I'll trim them to a finish and I'll trim
    them to a stand,

Till an honest glass of whiskey is a stranger
    in the land.

And the 'shakes' and 'snakes' and 'jim-jams'
    and 'delirium tremens' too
Ain't a marker or a circumstance to either
    one of you,
And I'll pay that thousand dollars, and re-
    spect the license clan,
Though for every dollar that I pay I'll have
    to kill a man."—*Nazarene Messenger.*

JESUS HAD THE KEY.

A negro on the shores of the river Bonny, in Africa, was condemned to death for having listened to the teachings of the missionaries and given up the worship of idols. At the last moment he was told that his life should be spared if he would return to idolatry. With great calmness he replied, "It's impossible for me to turn back to heathen worship for Jesus has taken charge of my heart and padlocked it to Himself. The key is with Him, so you see it is impossible for me to undo it without Him."—*Christian Advocate.*

www.ingramcontent.com/pod-product-compliance
Lightning Source LLC
Chambersburg PA
CBHW021159020426
42331CB00003B/131